Beth......,

- *resurrected church*

Richard Spencer and Adam Threlfall

Preview Version

Holy Trinity Church

Belle Vue Road, Shrewsbury, SY3 7LL, UK

Tel: 01743 244891, email: htbv@htbv.org.uk

.

Unless indicated otherwise, Bible passages are taken from the *New International Version*

Front cover illustration by Bożena Spencer

G025-25

Contents

Introduction

This book is a record of a conversation between Jesus and part of his bride – one local church: Holy Trinity Church, Belle Vue (HTBV), Shrewsbury, in the county of Shropshire. We will follow this conversation over a number of years, as he revealed more and more of his vision for his church. He said to the man who would be the first among the first apostles, "I will build my church", and we will follow how he has been building us into a worshiping fellowship that we hope more faithfully re-presents him to the world.

Let's start in the most obvious place in thinking about the church: Ephesians 5:21-32. Paul tells us that **'the church submits to Christ'** (v24) as a wife to her husband. It would be a strange marriage if, after the wedding day, the husband put a book of rules on the table, told his wife to obey them, and never spoke to her again. If Jesus loves the church in the way that this passage asserts, then if we do not hear him speaking, something is badly wrong.

If this book were the history of an earthly relationship, you would not expect every conversation between the parties to be recorded, just those that had a significant impact on their life together. Therefore, although we believe we have heard the voice of our Lord many times over these last few years, in these pages, you will find those revelations that led us to take major steps in our response to his love. Virtually all of the prophetic words recorded here were accompanied by some kind of confirmation, either through another believer, or through the pages of the Bible, or through circumstances, or a combination of these. Our previous books included testimonies of many remarkable healings and other miracles that we have experienced, but here we focus on revelation.

This book is arranged in three parts: Courtship, Proposal, Marriage. The name change to *Bethany* comes in the Proposal section; but one event that happened in Bethany in Judea needs to be mentioned at the outset. We believe that the raising of Lazarus is a real picture of what we have gone through in the last few years. Lazarus died of what was wrong with him because no-one healed him. Churches that conform to 'the pattern of the age' (Romans 12:2) are inherently unhealthy; Holy Trinity Church has effectively died and been raised to new life. We were given a prophetic word (which was amazingly confirmed): '*This is why Jesus delays, he is not here to fix up the church, but to resurrect it*' (see page 64). To use the terminology of Frank Viola[1], an institutional church has died and an organic church has risen in its place. This is its story.

Acknowledgements

Our grateful thanks must go to everyone mentioned in this book, but there are many more who have spoken out revelations, who have moved decisively in response to a prophetic word, who have remained faithful in fellowship, who have ministered or received healing, who have brought others into the kingdom, who have abandoned themselves in worship, who have revealed more of the Christ who is living in them. We are profoundly grateful to every one of them. A special thanks to Elizabeth Pike, Paul Kelly and others for their editorial efforts; but the remaining errors, typos, bad grammar, etc. are completely our responsibility.

---

[1] See for example: Viola, Frank. *Finding Organic Church: A Comprehensive Guide to Starting and Sustaining Authentic Christian Communities* David C Cook, 2009.

Courtship

Water flowing through the church

In the summer of 2006 we had our last stab at what you might call conventional evangelism. We hired a powerful professional evangelist to speak at a week of events (treasure hunts, quizzes, etc.) which we put on to attract members of our community. Although we worked our socks off and over 400 people heard our speaker, the week seemed fruitless; except that, in the weeks beforehand, we got together every Sunday evening to pray and worship in preparation for what we hoped would a great time of outreach. On one of those evenings I was sitting at the piano on the platform in church when I suddenly saw a sheet of water moving across the platform and down the central aisle. I asked Verity Lowe, who was standing at the lectern, if she knew where in the Book of Ezekiel, the account of the water flowing out of the Temple could be found. She looked down at the Bible in front of her and it was open to Ezekiel 47.

This passage could have been written about our building, which has its 'holy' end at the west (just like the Temple in Jerusalem) and has a permanent spring in the subterranean boiler room on the south side (see Ezekiel 47:2), so strong that it has worn out several pumps. I prayed about Ezekiel 47:1-12 and I believe the Lord said:

It is a passage with lots of meaning. For you (as a church) it means that my Spirit will flow out from you and you need to go where the Spirit is bringing new life. I have a purpose for you – to be the source of that living stream and to bring in the harvest that it produces. Pray for an outpouring of my Spirit.

This means that churches can be like individual Christians, with the Holy Spirit flowing out of them:

> John 7:37-39 **On the last and greatest day of the Feast, Jesus stood and said in a loud voice, "If anyone is thirsty, let him come to me and drink. Whoever believes in me, as the Scripture has said, streams of living water will flow from within him." By this he meant the Spirit, whom those who believed in him were later to receive. Up to that time the Spirit had not been given, since Jesus had not yet been glorified.**

As a postscript, in October 2012, John Coles, the Director of New Wine, preached in the church on an identical vision of a river flowing down the central aisle. He called for people who needed healing to step into this visionary river; Mary Parry did so and was immediately and permanently healed of a painful arthritic condition in her hands. She went from them always being bandaged to having full, pain-free use of them[2].

See what I can do!

In the autumn of 2006, I asked the celebrated Bible scholar Dick (R.T.) France to come and deliver a series of talks on the first four chapters of Matthew's Gospel. At that time, Dick was just completing his second commentary on Matthew's Gospel[3] and the four talks gave us wonderful insights into the early years of Jesus' life on earth. The fourth talk should have been on Friday 1st December, but Dick asked for the date to be slipped by a week. I

---

[2] Ezekiel 47:12

[3] RT France, *The Gospel of Matthew (New International Commentary on the New Testament)*, William B Eerdmans, 2007

forgot this and publicised and arranged the talk for the original date. We all turned up on that Friday evening and Laura Barratt, our Worship Leader, led us in worship, as on the previous evenings. Time went on and at 8pm, Dick had not arrived, so I phoned him to discover my mistake. I returned to church and apologised – there was nothing else we could do but continue to worship. Then God showed up! For the first time, we experienced an overwhelming sense of his presence. It was as if he was saying, "See what happens when you get to the end of your own resources, when you let me take charge." That sense of his presence has never left us as we come together in worship week by week. We could see why our absolute priority must always be the worship of God.

It is not an exaggeration to say that the talks that Dick France gave us were probably the best pieces of Bible exposition that I have ever heard. I believe that God was showing us that what he can provide is even better than the most godly, inspired, gifted, intelligent,… offering of man.

"Jesus wants to lead his church directly"

In 2007, I was praying for Holy Trinity Church with a group who were training to take on leadership roles in a number of different churches. One of the group suddenly blurted out:

"Jesus wants to lead his church directly".

I prayed about this and I believe that God said to me:

Jesus needs to be all in all for my plan of redemption to be complete. Your job is to persuade and to help people to let Jesus in. He needs direct access to his people.

As a 'church leader' it pains me to acknowledge that we are probably the major problem for the church in this country. We have so many vested interests that work against Jesus being the head of his church in practice and not just as a phrase from the Bible. We hate giving up control to him because it means we may not be able to do the things that please the people. Our jobs are, at least in part, dependent on our ability to deliver the goods; most notably to fill our churches with people who are willing to give. If we are not in charge, what security do we have?

In general, I do not watch the 'reality' programmes on television, but the BBC have come up with an idea that, in reality, is very insightful. The programme is called, 'Don't tell the Bride'; each week we see what happens when a prospective bridegroom is given a substantial amount of money to plan out every detail of his forthcoming wedding on condition that the bride knows nothing until the wedding day. The question is, of course, does the bride have sufficient faith and trust in her future husband to leave him to organise what she hopes will be the greatest day of her life? All the programmes I have seen have happy endings, with each bride's faith in her future husband being fully justified – each one had a wonderful time, even though it was not what she would have planned for herself[4]. The valuable lesson in these programmes is that the key thing is faith in a *person*; not in a plan, a doctrine, a concept or anything else abstract or inanimate.

To let Jesus lead his church directly, the human leadership of the church often needs to get out of the way. The leader's role should focus on helping all the members of the body connect directly with the head, and ensuring that the spiritual environment is not compromised.

---

[4] Possibly, the disasters when the bride is really disappointed are never aired.

"Manifestation, not representation"

It is a characteristic of Jesus as revealed in the Gospels, that he never says or does what you would expect; and his timing, though always perfect is also invariably surprising. So it was with this word that I received in the loudest part of the worship at the youth camp, Soul Survivor, in the summer of 2007:

"Manifestation, not representation."

That may seem a bit of a mouthful, but the meaning is fairly clear. If we give up on trying to represent the presence of God (through 'religious' activities) then he will manifest (i.e. make real in our experience) his actual presence.

The Holy Spirit led us to see a contrast between two passages that are linked in the Bible: the Golden Calf and the Day of Pentecost. Before we look at the contrast we need to see how these two passages are linked together.

• When the Israelites worshipped the Golden Calf about 3,000 people were killed[5], on the Day of Pentecost about 3,000 were saved and baptised[6].

• At Pentecost, the Jews have always celebrated the encounter with God at Sinai as described in the Book of Exodus, and in particular, receiving the Ten Commandments and the rest of the Law.

• Just before each of these passages, the leader of the people (Moses, Jesus) went up to meet with God and was covered by a

---

[5] Exodus 32:28

[6] Acts 2:41

12

cloud[7]. In each case they left the second-in-command (Aaron, Peter) in charge.

We need to be clear that in worshipping the Golden Calf, they had not found a new god for themselves or taken up the worship of the Egyptians. They made a representation of the God who had saved them.

> Exodus 32:4-5 (NASB) *Aaron* took *their gold rings* from their hand, and fashioned it with a graving tool and made it into a molten calf; and they said, "This is your god, O Israel, who brought you up from the land of Egypt." Now when Aaron saw this, he built an altar before it; and Aaron made a proclamation and said, "Tomorrow shall be a feast to the Lord."

The contrast is clear in the fruit of these actions: 3,000 deaths vs. 3,000 new births. The difference is so stark that it is self-evident that we have to do everything we can to move to the latter. The Golden Calf represents what we might call representational worship, which clearly is an anathema to God.

So how should we worship God? The Day of Pentecost tells us that God is looking for worship that:

- Is completely 'vertical', focussing on him and ignoring the 'needs' and desires of the worshippers.
- Involves no human-created representations of his presence.
- Is initiated and led by the Holy Spirit and therefore is unpredictable[8] and spontaneous, rather than pre-planned and programmed.

---

[7] See Exodus 19:20, Exodus 20:21, John 20:17, Acts 1:9

[8] Jesus said to Nicodemus (a teacher of Israel), **"The wind blows wherever it pleases. You hear its sound, but you cannot tell where it comes from or where it is going. So it is with everyone born of the Spirit."** (John 3:8)

13

- Is completely truthful and authentic, and therefore has an impact on those outside the community of faith.
- Is willing to wait on him.
- Will spill out into the world.

Representational worship is when we believe something under our control is the essence of God's presence with us. A fairly obvious example is the Catholic mass, where the bread and wine are said to actually be the body and blood of Jesus, i.e. he is said to be present on the altar when the priest says the required words. Less obvious is the way the sermon is treated in some churches, as if it were the only way that God can speak to the congregation. In other churches, the liturgy is sacrosanct – to the extent that correct repetition is what is needed for God to be with us. Even charismatic prayer ministry can take the place of a direct encounter with God, if people put their faith in being prayed for, rather than in the one being prayed to.

It has been our experience in worship that, if we consciously give up trying to represent God's presence with us, then he will make himself manifestly known.

To summarise, a non-negotiable statement:

Worship, pre-planned to please the people, using a representation of God's presence brings condemnation and death. Spontaneous, Holy-Spirit led worship (focussed only on God) brings signs, wonders, revelations and new life in abundance.

Apostolic Team

On 27th July 2009, one of our young people, Craig Silcock, who had spent several months working in South Africa with Soul Action spoke about the 'Apostolic' leadership of the church there, based on the five ministries listed in Ephesians 4:11: Apostles, Prophets, Evangelists, Pastors and Teachers. To be perfectly honest, we had never even thought about this kind of leadership for HTBV, although we now realise how significant this is in the current move of God. That evening, during the loudest part of the worship at Soul Survivor, God gave me five names corresponding to the five ministries. I realised he was telling me to set up an Apostolic Team to replace the Local Ministry Team (LMT) which the church had elected just a few months earlier. The LMT graciously agreed to disband itself in favour of the new Team and this was unanimously ratified at the next meeting of the Parochial Church Council (PCC), the legal body in the church.

God gave me my own name as an apostle to HTBV. This probably merits some explanation. The word 'apostle' comes directly from the Greek word *apostolos*, which is not a 'religious' word, but just means a person who is sent on behalf of someone else, a messenger. Jesus could have called the twelve, 'patriarchs', 'priests' or 'prophets' or even 'kings', all of which would have clarified their roles by connecting them to Old Testament figures, but he chose a new term, perhaps because he knew he would be saying to them after the Resurrection:

John 20:21 **...Jesus said, "Peace be with you! As the Father has sent me, I am sending you."**

So an apostle is someone Jesus sends out. I believe Jesus did send my wife Bozy and me to HTBV and the evidence for this goes back into the 1980's. I came to faith in 1985, and a year later Bozy and I attended an evening service at HTBV, at the end of which, the then Vicar, Paul James, came up to me and asked, "Are you a clergyman?" I, of course, answered in the negative, nothing was further from my mind, the computer company four of my friends and I had started in 1981 was just beginning to really get going. Later, however, I did receive a call from God to full-time ministry, but this was not until late 1991 (also in Shrewsbury). By 1999 I was reaching the end of my three years as a curate (assistant minister) in Leek, and we heard that there was a vacancy at HTBV. Remembering Paul James' words, I applied for the job, sensing that God was in this. When I came for the interview, there was one more piece of confirmation. One of the interview panel, appointed by the patrons of the church, was a retired vicar named Martin Peppiatt. Martin and I had had a five-hour conversation about the Christian faith in 1985, just before I came to faith, a conversation I still remember to this day. God used these two godly men to confirm that he was sending us to HTBV – in that sense I believe I can claim an apostolic calling to this church.

I realised that the other four names were our most gifted prophet, evangelist, pastor and teacher – apostolic leadership is characterised by God's gifting. This is clear at the place where the five-fold ministry is introduced in the Bible:

Ephesians 4:7-11 **But to each one of us grace has been given as Christ apportioned it. This is why it says: "When he ascended on high, he led captives in his train and gave gifts to men." (What does "he ascended" mean except that he also descended to the lower, earthly region. He who descended is the very one who ascended higher than all the heavens, in order to fill the whole universe.) It was he who gave some to be apostles, some to be prophets, some to be evangelists, and some to be pastors and teachers...**

When we come to faith in Jesus, the Father places us in him. As he is seated at the Father's right hand, so we are with him in heaven[9]. While we are with him he gives us gifts, and he sends us back to earth with himself living in us. Each of us receives part of his gifting, so that we can together, truly re-present here and now (for more on this please see page 36).

---

[9]   Ephesians 2:6

Bread from heaven vision and "Living together in the presence of God"

On 17th December 2009, at exactly the same moment I was given this phrase to be a mission statement for the church: 'Living together in the Presence of God', Laura Barratt, our Worship Leader, was given this vision:

> *"I saw lots of people on top of a mountain. I could see their eyes looking up to heaven and their hands raised. As they did this I saw God give each one a loaf of bread. Each loaf was different (shape/size etc) as it represented the different ways in which God speaks to His people. Each person would take their loaf and break it and share it with one another. The bread they were given and were sharing was always fresh. We need to feed each other with what God has given us. It needs to come straight from God as it is REAL food and is what we and others need. We need to live and depend on fresh revelation."*

This vision has sustained us ever since. It has more Biblical support than any other prophetic statement I have ever heard, these are just some of the Bible passages that resonate with it: Genesis 22:13-14; Exodus 16:4..18-20; Leviticus 24:8; Isaiah 55:2-3; Nehemiah 9:15; Matthew 4:4; Matthew 12:3-4; Luke 11:3; Luke 22:19; Luke 24:30-31; John 6:27,32-33,35,51-56; Acts 2:46; Acts 3:6; 1 Corinthians 12:7-8. It is a promise that we do not need to take bread for the journey[10], we can depend on receiving revelation when we need it, either directly from heaven or through another of God's children.

---

[10] Luke 9:3

Train vision

In April 2010, one of our church members, Steve Johnson, had this vision:

I saw the inside of the building. The walls and ceiling were the same, but instead of pews there was a train and a platform. It was a steam train. It was bright and shiny, with lots of noise and steam. There were people on the train. A driver and chief engineer aboard the engine. People in first, second and third class. There were even people who had sneaked into the baggage car. People who really had no right to be on board, but were intent on riding the train no matter what! Everybody seemed happy and excited to be there. Just waiting for the train to leave. Wondering what they would see on the way.

Then I saw another group. Standing on the platform. Each had a train ticket in their hand. A ticket to ride. Ready to get on board, but not doing it. Just looking at them made me feel sad. They had everything they needed to get on the train. They had the right to get on board – they just wouldn't. They weren't sure where the train was going. How long would the journey be? What if they didn't like it? Could they get off if they changed their mind?

While they were standing there, the train started to pull out of the station. Very slowly at first. They could still get on board if they wished – if they were quick. Then the train picked up speed and it was too late.

Then I heard a wail. Very loud. Like someone crying for a child that is dead or missing. It was not the people who had missed the train – it was God crying for them![11]

---

[11]   Steve Johnson, 25th April 2010

What Steve did not know at the time was that my children had bought me, as a birthday present, the opportunity to spend a day learning to be a steam engine driver and a fireman. It was clear that God was speaking to the church through Steve, that the church was moving and they had the choice whether to get on it or be left behind.

Chris Overstreet's prophecy

On the evening of 19th September 2010 a chain of events started that were to have profound implications for HTBV. I had decided to show the previous Sunday evening service from Bethel Church on the big screen in the hall. Bethel offer an Internet facility allowing subscribers to stream video from any of their services and conferences (ibethel.tv), and in this Sunday evening service Bill Johnson was speaking about *Christ in you, the hope of glory*[12]. A few of us listened to the talk and then watched the following ministry time, where a young man stood up and gave a very specific word of knowledge. He said that there was someone who had had a serious injury to their right wrist 3½ years ago in the month of March, which had left them with a physical scar. God wanted to heal this person from the effects of the trauma caused by this accident. This applied almost exactly to one of our members sitting there, Maggie McCormack, who showed us a large cross-shaped scar on her wrist and told us how she nearly bled to death when she put her arm through a pane of glass. So we stopped the video stream and prayed for healing from trauma for Maggie. We sent the Media Director, Tim Jenné, at ibethel.tv an email as a testimony and added it to our list of signs and wonders.

The next day I showed the same video to another church member, Josie Owen-Roberts, who was not with us the previous

---

[12]   Colossians 1:27

evening. She recognised the young man giving the word of knowledge as Chris Overstreet[13], the Outreach Pastor at Bethel, and then she added to my amazement by saying that he was coming to Telford (the next town to Shrewsbury) the following week to speak at a conference on Supernatural Evangelism. I contacted the organisers of the conference to book places and to ask if Chris might be free on the next Sunday to come and preach at HTBV. That Sunday was a turning point in the life of the church – Chris spoke and then he and two friends, Steve Rademan and Thomas Harry, prayed individually for almost the whole congregation as they came forward. We had a number of healings that morning (including a long-term problem with migraines) and these have continued ever since – some of the testimonies are in this book. Chris also gave us a word of prophecy, which has sustained us in these following years:

> *I saw this place filled with people that were passionately on fire for Jesus. I sensed in my heart that the Lord is going to do a move, He wants to move into this area. The Lord Jesus, He wants to take occupation, to take over this area.*

> *I felt the Lord is going to begin to move upon hearts, that there is going to be a new fire come into hearts and a release of a desire to communicate to other people.*

> *In my heart I saw this place filled with worship. I saw the gifts of the Holy Spirit moving amongst people. I saw where the gifts of the Holy Spirit moving through individual lives, like yourself. There was an excitement that was in hearts, a thriving. I saw young people, I saw old people. I just saw this place packed out.*

> *I saw extended meetings; I saw a spirit of revival coming into this*

---

[13] See Chris' book on Jesus' way of evangelism: Chris Overstreet, *A Practical Guide to Evangelism Supernaturally*, Destiny Image, 2011

place, where the Lord was actually going to fill this place with His glory.

I believe that if you do your history, about 1909-11 something began to take place in this area. God wants to do a visitation, not just a visitation but a habitation in this place, where His presence becomes the theme in this church.

I feel in my heart that there is such a love that you have for the Lord already. I could feel the love of the Father for you. I could feel two hearts colliding together. God's heart for you, and your heart for Him. Two hearts colliding together which creates fire, which creates momentum. I believe that the Lord is, if you will, going to reproduce fire in your life. He's going to reproduce the passion that you're carrying right now.

There's a reproducing, a reproduction of passion and fire that I'm sensing the Lord wants to do. God is going to do an amazing thing in your life.[14]

We have tried to track down the reference to something happening in the years 1909-11 and have come up with two possibilities (which may be connected). The first concerns two *American* evangelists who met for the first time in April 1911 in Shrewsbury: J. Wilbur Chapman and John 'Praying' Hyde. Chapman had been invited to lead a series of evangelistic rallies in Shrewsbury Music Hall, the main theatre in the town. These proved to be a great disappointment, so Chapman called a meeting of the town's church leaders. They turned out to be as unenthusiastic as the general population, but John Hyde was taken to the meeting by one of the ministers and made a commitment to support Chapman in prayer, saying, "I cannot leave a brother minister to bear this

---

[14] Prophetic word by Chris Overstreet, Outreach Pastor of Bethel Church, Redding, California for Holy Trinity Church 3rd October 2010

burden alone." The change in the effectiveness of Chapman's evangelistic ministry was immediate and dramatic; fifty people came to faith on the next night alone. The two men had private prayer times about which Chapman later recalled, "I felt the hot tears running down my face. I knew that we had entered into the presence of God." Hyde put his arm around Chapman's shoulders, "There came up from the depths of his heart such petitions for men as I have never heard before, and I rose from my knees to know what real prayer was." [15]

The second possibility of things happening in Shrewsbury in 1909-11 is that it seems clear that this is the timeframe when the outflow from the Welsh Revival (1904-5) reached the town and when the first Pentecostal churches were established. Written records are sketchy, but there is an account of Smith Wigglesworth preaching at Pontesbury, a village close to Shrewsbury, in 1908[16]. HTBV has a very close relationship with Wellspring Church across Belle Vue Road, part of the Apostolic Church, an international denomination that grew out of the Welsh Revival. There is some evidence to suggest that this church was founded around the years 1909-11. I believe God is saying that he wants to do something as radical today as the Welsh Revival and the Azusa Street Revival a century ago. Because God is infinitely creative, he never repeats himself, but he does build on what he has done before, so we are praying for God to move just as powerfully today as he did at the start of the 20th Century.

The Three Signs of Revival

As we have seen, Jesus is happy to confirm his prophetic words to us, but we have to allow him to choose the means by

---

[15] Paul Mershon, *Getting Hold of God,*, March 2010

[16] Letter by G.E. Beady in *Confidence Magazine*, November 1908

which he gives us the confidence to act on what we believe we have heard from him. Although he never needs to repeat himself, sometimes he communicates using which might be called parallel paths. Over the last few years, God has spoken to me three times in the same way, by giving me book, chapter and verse from the Bible. The common factor seems to be a promise of revival. The three verses are:

Hosea 6:2 **After two days he will revive us; on the third day he will restore us, that we may live in his presence.**

John 2:1 **On the third day a wedding took place at Cana in Galilee. Jesus' mother was there,**

Luke 7:8 **"For I myself am a man under authority, with soldiers under me. I tell this one, 'Go', and he goes; and that one, 'Come', and he comes. I say to my servant, 'Do this', and he does it."**

Hosea 6:2

Hosea 6:2 **After two days he will revive us; on the third day he will restore us, that we may live in his presence.**

I believe God gave me this verse (and confirmed it very clearly) on 7th March 2009. The Hebrew word translated *days* and *day* here is the same word (*yom*) that is used in Genesis 1 for the seven *days* of creation. It has been pointed out many times that this word, in Hebrew, can mean a year or an indeterminate period of time, in fact it is the only word available in Hebrew for a period of time. This verse seems to be a promise that, after a waiting time, we can expect revival (or new life), restoration (or being lifted up) and on-going life in the presence of God. Some years later, Jesus spoke to us again about being willing to wait for him to move, see page 64.

John 2:1

John 2:1 **On the third day a wedding took place at Cana in Galilee. Jesus' mother was there,**

On 7th July 2010 God gave me this verse at a meeting. For the third year running, our Children's Leader, Sandra Lloyd, had been asked to head up one of the children's groups at that year's New Wine camp at Shepton Mallet. We knew we would be working with up to 400 children and adults, and Sandra, had prepared a presentation of a New Testament story for each of five days at the camp. At the very end of the very last preparation meeting, as we were praying, God said to me 'John Chapter 2 Verse 1'. We looked at the verse in the Bible and we looked at each other and realised that we needed to tell the story of the Wedding at Cana on the third of the five days, rather than what had been planned – Philip and the Ethiopian[17] (the only passage *we* had chosen that was not from the Gospels). Sandra did not complain but, in the few days remaining, prepared a totally new presentation for the third day of New Wine.

The question is: What does this have to do with revival? The most obvious connection is that the Wedding of Cana had some of the hallmarks of revival. The last verse of this passage is:

John 2:11 **This, the first of his miraculous signs, Jesus performed at Cana in Galilee. He thus revealed his glory, and his disciples put their faith in him.**

The glory of God is manifested and a significant number of people come to faith in Jesus – this is what is seen in revivals. We pray for the presence of Jesus within us to be manifested in signs and wonders, and for many people to put their trust in him.

It is curious that Jesus' two, what we might call, 'creative', miracles (water into wine and the feeding of the five thousand[18]) are clearly related. Both started with 'natural ingredients', i.e. with what had been provided by ordinary means, and both produced enough for the same number of people[19]. The connection with communion is clear. Jesus is saying that whenever he asks us to do anything ("Do this in remembrance of me"[20]) he will always provide whatever we need.

Luke 7:8

On 8th December 2010, I had this conversation with God:

Me: Move in unmistakeable power, Lord. Show everyone that you are at work to bring revival to us. What will be the sign of this?

God: My sign is this - Luke Chapter 7 verse 8.

Luke 7:8 **"For I myself am a man under authority, with soldiers under me. I tell this one 'Go', and he goes; and that one, 'Come', and he comes. I say to my servant, 'Do this', and he does it".**

In context:

Luke 7

1 **When Jesus had finished saying all this in the hearing of the people, he entered Capernaum. 2 There a centurion's servant, whom his master valued highly, was sick and about to die. 3 The centurion heard of Jesus and sent some elders of the Jews to him, asking him to come and heal his servant. 4 When they came to Jesus, they pleaded earnestly with him, "This man deserves to have you do this, 5 because**

---

[18] John 6:1-14

[19] When Jesus turned the water into wine, John 2:6 indicates that he produced enough to fill about 5,000 cups.

[20] Luke 22:19

he loves our nation and has built our synagogue." 6 So Jesus went with them. He was not far from the house when the centurion sent friends to say to him: "Lord, don't trouble yourself, for I do not deserve to have you come under my roof. 7 That is why I did not even consider myself worthy to come to you. But say the word, and my servant will be healed. 8 For I myself am a man under authority, with soldiers under me. I tell this one, 'Go', and he goes; and that one, 'Come', and he comes. I say to my servant, 'Do this', and he does it." 9 When Jesus heard this, he was amazed at him, and turning to the crowd following him, he said, "I tell you, I have not found such great faith even in Israel." 10 Then the men who had been sent returned to the house and found the servant well.

There is no clear connection between this verse and the outpouring of the power of God that we associate with the word 'revival', so it was obvious that I needed some more revelation to unpack this. Subsequently, God spoke again in ways that helped me to understand the significance of the Centurion's statement.

The Centurion's Authority

Jesus was amazed at the Centurion's faith. He had real insight into Jesus' authority and the way that Jesus exercised the power that he had been given. An officer in any army gets things done by speaking – he issues orders and expects them to be obeyed without question. The Centurion could see, by analogy with his own situation, that Jesus was able to get things done by speaking orders to the creation (i.e. to the forces of nature, the physical universe). He knew that Jesus could heal his servant just by saying a word.

Jesus told us to follow him, and that we would do even greater things than him (John 14:12). In Luke 7:8 we see how we are to do this; we are officers in his army, we can issue orders to the world that he made and expect them to be obeyed. This should not surprise us, most of the miracles in the Gospels and the Acts happen by Jesus or the Apostles giving orders. For example, in the next passage after Luke 7:1-10, Jesus speaks to a dead body:

Luke 7:14 **Then *Jesus* went up and touched the coffin, and those carrying it stood still. He said, "Young man, I say to you, get up!"**

This principle of issuing commands to the physical universe goes right back to the beginning of creation.

Hebrews 11:3 **By faith we understand that the universe was formed at God's command, so that what is seen was not made out of what was visible.**

But this does not just apply to God.

Genesis 1:27-28 **So God created man in his own image, in the image of God he created him; male and female he created them. God blessed them and said to them, "Be fruitful and increase in number; fill the earth and subdue it. Rule over the fish of the sea and the birds of the air and over every living creature that moves on the ground."**

The question is, how was mankind to exercise power in subduing the earth? The answer comes in the next chapter.

Genesis 2:19-20 **Now the LORD God had formed out of the ground all the beasts of the field and all the birds of the air. He brought them to the man to see what he would name them; and whatever the man called each living creature, that was its name.**

Adam was told to give the animals names so that he could command them. There is a pale reflection of this in the way we give names to our domestic animals and train them to respond to spoken commands. It is clear that mankind was intended to have dominion over the creation simply by speaking to it. But of course, everything went wrong at the Fall.

Genesis 3:17-19 **To Adam he said, "Because you listened to your wife and ate from the tree about which I commanded you, 'You must not eat of it,' Cursed is the ground because of you; through painful toil you will eat of it all the days of your life. It will produce thorns and thistles for you, and you will eat the plants of the field. By the sweat of your brow you will eat your food until you return to the ground,** since from it you were taken; for dust you are and to dust you will return."

To use the military analogy, Adam and Eve were demoted from being officers that could get things done by giving orders, to enlisted soldiers who would have to do all the work themselves.

In the Old Testament, God showed the prophets the power of the prophetic word:

Ezekiel 37:4-5 Then he said to me, "Prophesy to these bones and say to them, 'Dry bones, hear the word of the LORD! This is what the Sovereign LORD says to these bones: I will make breath enter you, and you will come to life...'"

Ezekiel spoke to the dry bones twice and a whole army came into being; he really was an officer in the Lord's army! In the New Testament, we see how the Acts of the Apostles were accomplished:

Acts 3:6-7 Then Peter said *to the crippled man*, "Silver or gold I do not have, but what I have I give you. In the name of Jesus Christ of Nazareth, walk." Taking him by the right hand, he helped him up, and instantly the man's feet and ankles became strong.

A Man under Authority

There is another aspect of Luke 7:8 that helps to put this in context. In a different translation:

Luke 7:7-8 (TNIV) "...Just say the word from where you are, and my servant will be healed. I know this because I am under the authority of my superior officers, and I have authority over my soldiers. I only need to say, 'Go,' and they go, or 'Come,' and they come. And if I say to my slaves, 'Do this,' they do it."

The Centurion saw that Jesus was submitted to the Father's authority, just as he came under the authority of those in command over him. He recognised the source of his own authority in his willingness to accept the orders of his superior officers. Jesus was astounded by this man because he understood Jesus' submission and because of it he was willing to put *real* faith in him. When Jesus said to the disciples, "Follow me", he meant it; and Luke 7:8 shows us how we are to 'do our bit' in the cosmic war with the forces of evil.

The British Armed Forces have a rule book called *Queen's Regulations*. Every officer needs to be familiar with it, but, if he or she is to play their vital part in the conduct of a war they need to receive and act on the orders that come down the chain of command, when they receive them. As Christians we have our equivalent to *Queen's Regulations*, the Bible, but without a steady stream of up-to-date communications from our Commander-in-Chief we will never be effective in pushing back the forces of evil from our world. This is where Luke 7:8 speaks about revival. Revivals are like major campaigns in the conduct of a war, they are times when the enemy's hold on a region is overcome. Think of Operation Overlord in the Second World War: this started on D-Day and resulted in the capture of a large part of Normandy; and then think of the Welsh Revival in 1904-5 when it is estimated that 100,000 became Christians. God needs people who are willing to think, speak and act like the Centurion; who will be his Local Commanders in the field, listening for orders and speaking out commands over the forces of evil and the forces of nature.

The need for secure communications in warfare is evident. I worked in the 1990's for the Royal Navy on the systems used to send orders to submarines. The messages sent are very highly encrypted to ensure that any potential enemy can neither read them nor alter them. God continues to speak to his people, but he needs us to exercise the gift of discernment and to use *King's Regulations* to check[21] out what we receive. There is considerable evidence that our enemy cannot hear what God is saying to us, but he may be able to work out what our Commander's plans are from what we say and do. For example, it appears that the devil was unaware of the arrival of the Messiah on planet Earth until the Magi spoke to Herod. The devil characteristically over-reacted by getting Herod to kill all the baby boys in Bethlehem (Matthew 2:16). The devil's plans were thwarted when Local Commander Joseph received his orders in a dream to take Mary and Jesus to Egypt (Matthew 2:13).

The Bible is quite clear that we are at war with the forces of evil:

Genesis 3:15 *God said to the serpent, "...And I will put enmity between you and the woman, and between your offspring and hers; he will crush your head, and you will strike his heel."*

There is no doubt of the outcome of this war, the crushing of the devil's head, but we may sustain injuries, as Jesus did, from his attacks in the meantime.

Mark 1:23-26 **Just then a man in their synagogue who was possessed by an evil spirit cried out, "What do you want with us, Jesus of Nazareth? Have you come to destroy us? I know who you are—the Holy One of God!" "Be quiet!" said Jesus sternly. "Come out of him!" The evil spirit shook the man violently and came out of him with a shriek.**

The demons know what Jesus can do through his words to them.

Luke 10:18 **Jesus replied, "I saw Satan fall like lightning from heaven..."**

---

[21] The Bible also tells us about the conduct of the war in the past and gives us some insights into our Commander's strategic planning, but we continue to need day-by-day and even minute-by-minute tactical commands.

Jesus said this after he had sent out the 72 disciples with a very specific set of orders to exercise authority over diseases and tell the population under enemy occupation that the kingdom of God was at hand (Luke 10:1-11), i.e. that the front line of God's advancing army would soon get to them.

Romans 16:20 **The God of peace will soon crush Satan under your feet.**

God's promise to us is the same as at the beginning.

Hebrews 2:14 **Since the children have flesh and blood, he too shared in their humanity so that by his death he might destroy him who holds the power of death – that is, the devil...**

Jesus' death on the cross was the battle that turned the war. The devil thought he was getting rid of Jesus by having him executed as a common criminal. The killing of Aslan in *The Lion, the Witch and the Wardrobe* is a powerful allegory of this. Little did the devil realise that Jesus would be born in everyone who puts their trust in him – satan now faces a whole army of *Little Christs* (to use C.S. Lewis' term from *Mere Christianity*).

1 John 3:8 **The reason the Son of God appeared was to destroy the devil's work.**

We can also say that the reason that the Son of God lives in us and manifests his presence through us is to win this war completely.

There are few points of clarification necessary:

1. We cannot deny that it is possible to be deceived in what we think God is saying. Ultimately, this depends on our relationship with him. The better we know him the more reliably we will be able to discern what we are hearing; but he does allow us to start with 'a few things' and then he will entrust us with more (Matthew 25:23).

2. We do not need to be concerned with what other centurions are doing. In the conduct of a war, the commander-in-chief may need his local commanders to do different things, for example, to create a pincer movement he needs forces to move in opposite directions. Therefore it may be working against God's plans for us to copy what another apparently successful ministry is doing – we need our own orders.

3. Final victory is assured at the Last Day, but Jesus was emphatic that

Mark 13:32 **"No-one knows about that day or hour, not even the angels in heaven, nor the Son, but only the Father."**

There are fairly obvious reasons why *we* do not need to know this, but it is interesting that this has been hidden from the enemy as well. This is clearly a good strategy; it means that all the theories of the rapture, amillennialism, premillennialism, postmillennialism, etc. are doing nothing more than keeping the devil guessing. Luke 7:8 helps us to realise that we do not need to know the overall plan, but each of us has a vital role in hastening the final inevitable outcome. We can clearly see the purpose of the church militant. Most theories about the end times relegate the church to a minor supporting role in God's great plan of redemption of the universe (see Romans 8:19-22), but we can now see how significant we are.

4. The centurion was concerned with tactics; those further up the chain of command were responsible for strategy. It is the same with us – God sets the strategy and decides how to use each local commander (i.e. you and me) as the war unfolds. We can so easily become a liability rather than an asset to him if we try to work out our own strategies or borrow them from the world, or even other churches. It is well worth reading 2 Chronicles Chapter 20 to see how God

set the strategy for King Jehoshaphat and the people of Judah when they were threatened with invasion. Jehoshaphat proclaimed a fast and brought all (specifically including the women and children) together in Jerusalem to seek the Lord. Jehoshaphat's prayer ended with these words:

2 Chronicles 20:12 **"...we have no power to face this vast army that is attacking us. We do not know what to do, but our eyes are upon you."**

God sent a prophet, Jahaziel, who relayed God's commands to them

2 Chronicles 20:17 **"...You will not have to fight this battle. Take up your positions; stand firm and see the deliverance the LORD will give you, O Judah and Jerusalem. Do not be afraid; do not be discouraged. Go out to face them tomorrow, and the LORD will be with you."**

Jehoshaphat's first tactical move on hearing this was to worship God. This was all that was necessary:

2 Chronicles 20:22 **As they began to sing and praise, the LORD set ambushes against the men of Ammon and Moab and Mount Seir who were invading Judah, and they were defeated.**

This is a great example of the strategic work of God that needs his people to have faith in him, and knowledge of him to be able to respond tactically. God is looking for people today who know the difference between strategy and tactics, who will resist the temptation to work out their own strategies, but who will thoughtfully respond in courage and faith to the orders they receive. Working in a strategy given by God means that he can draft in angelic forces so that together we can achieve far more than is humanly possible.

5. In the conduct of a war, the commander-in-chief will choose which troops to deploy based on his or her assessment of their capabilities. Any mission that has particular significance or risk will require those that have demonstrated their courage, faithfulness, integrity and intelligence. God will only use us powerfully if he knows we will receive and carry out his orders, sticking to his strategy. He may need us to display some tactical ingenuity, but this will always be within the bounds he has set.

The Centurion's authority was valid because he was submitted to those in authority over him; he had demonstrated his willingness to obey orders when he received them. Our authority over 'the world, the flesh and the devil' is dependent on us receiving and obeying commands from our commander-in-chief, dynamically. We cannot expect to have our commands obeyed in healing, deliverance, resistance to temptation and other interactions with the physical and demonic worlds, if we will not listen and step out in faith and obedience. Most churches believe they have authority over how they conduct worship, but we need to give this over to the Holy Spirit. Perhaps then, we will discover that we can command the forces that oppose us out in the world.

Seasonal Fruit

On the evening of 24th February 2011, Derek McCormack spoke out this prophecy:

I am about to give seasonal fruit, about to give fruit in season. I am about to rain down upon you seasonal fruits; fruits from my kingdom, new and fresh, from my heart. Giving you the desires of your heart. Your heart and my heart are meeting. I will reveal my heart to you. As I reveal my heart, I give you my seasonal fruit.

A week later I had a scheduled meeting with a colleague, Jeremy Oakley, as we were both following the same training course from Bethel Church, Redding, California. I read out the prophecy and to my surprise, Jeremy started speaking about conkers[22]. His memory from childhood was of having to wait for the right season to be able to harvest conkers to be able to use them in the time-honoured game. He pointed out that conkers are useless, in their tight prickly skins until they are ripe; then their skins turn brown and the conkers just fall out. I thanked him for his graphic description and thought no more about this; until the next day. I went to a church leaders' meeting at Preston Hall, near Shrewsbury. As we were sitting in a circle, I looked up and there were two watercolour paintings exactly illustrating Jeremy's description. These paintings are shown on the back cover of this book.

We are always impatient, and Jesus needs to remind us that we sometimes need to wait for the right season to see things happen. Just like the disciples between the Ascension and the Day of Pentecost we don't know how long, but we know that it will always be worth the wait.

Jesus said these words to me:

My heart is for you to just be, be in my presence, be my people, be at peace. It's the doing that leads you astray – to places where I do not want you to go. Unless you learn to be, I cannot trust you to do.

---

[22] The fruit of the horse chestnut tree.

The 'Christ in us – Us in Christ' Diagram

In the autumn of 2012, James Wade came up with this diagram. As we examined it, we realised that it contains a wealth of revelation. It shows graphically how the cross has enabled us to live in Christ (in heaven) and how he comes to live in us (here on earth).

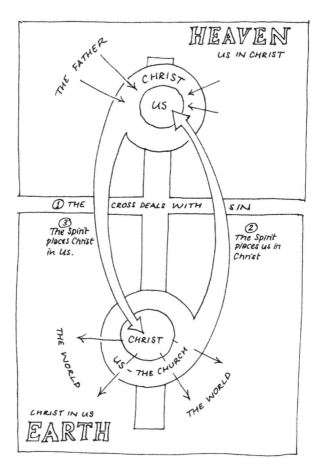

There is a curious symmetry here. The Father can see us in Christ; the world should be able to see Christ in us. We can communicate with the Father because we are resident in the Son; the Son wants to communicate to the world though the only part of his kingdom that the world can see: US!

W. Ian Thomas put this succinctly:

To be in Christ - that is redemption; but for Christ to be in you - that is sanctification! To be in Christ - that makes you fit for heaven; but for Christ to be in you - that makes you fit for earth! To be in Christ - that changes your destination; but for Christ to be in you - that changes your destiny! The one makes heaven your home - the other makes this world His workshop.[23]

CS Lewis understood this:

When Christians say the Christ-life is in them, they do not mean simply something mental or moral. When they speak of being "in Christ" or of Christ being "in them," this is not simply a way of saying that they are thinking about Christ or copying Him. They mean that Christ is actually operating through them...[24]

The life of Christ on earth, when he lived here in his own body, shows us what it means for you to be in Christ and for him to live in you. Jesus on earth, was in constant communion with the Father, yet at the same time, was ready in engage with anyone and

---

[23] W. Ian Thomas - *The Saving Life of Christ*,. page 19

[24] C. S. Lewis - *Mere Christianity.* pages 64,65

everyone. His 33 years is the complete model for us, and this drawing helps us to see how it can become a reality.

> **"I tell you the truth, anyone who has faith in me will do what I have been doing. He will do even greater things than these, because I am going to the Father."** (John 14:12)

Ian Thomas also wrote:

> *The Christian life is the life of the Lord Jesus Christ lived nineteen hundred years ago, lived now by Him in you!*[25]

If we consider the drawing again, we can appreciate that the upward arrow is composed of many people, who are placed in one body in heaven: Christ's. The downward arrow is one person, Christ, who is placed in many physical bodies, which make up one spiritual body: the church. This is the place of transformation as the members of this body are made into the likeness of the one who lives at their heart and is their head.

The verse in the Bible which seems to sum up the work of God in this season is this:

2 Corinthians 3:18 **And we, who with unveiled faces all reflect the Lord's glory, are being transformed into his likeness with ever-increasing glory, which comes from the Lord, who is the Spirit.**

The word translated 'reflect' actually means 'look at oneself in a mirror'. The verse is speaking about us recognising the presence of Jesus within us (looking in a mirror) and being transformed into his likeness. Hopefully, because we have an uncovered face, others can see his presence in us. The word 'faces' is actually in the singular, perhaps suggesting that the true likeness of Jesus can only

---

[25] W. Ian Thomas - *The Saving Life of Christ.* page 120

be seen in the church, rather than in any one individual, although some people do seem to radiate his glory. The goal for us as individuals and as a church is transparency, whilst eliminating non-Christlike attitudes and behaviour. What is certainly counter-productive is just trying to be a good person, or 'faking it'.

Some Questions

We have discovered that this diagram can help in answering some questions that arise when we consider how we can live in Christ and he in us.

1. When are we placed in Christ, and when does he come to live in us?

During the 20th Century there was much debate about whether the New Testament promises a 'second blessing', i.e. something that happens to Christians some time later than conversion. Some Pentecostals believe that the baptism of the Holy Spirit is available to us after we have come to faith, and we know this has happened when we receive the gift of tongues. Other Christians believe that we are given everything that is available to us in this life at the moment we come to faith[26].

We have discovered that the most common ways that the New Testament identifies Christians is that they are *in Christ* and that he is *in them*. Are these statements true about every believer the moment he or she comes to faith in Jesus, or should we expect these transformations to happen at some later point in the Christian life? We can find biblical examples to support a range of opinions; therefore this is probably something we need to leave to God. He

---

[26] See this book for a clear explanation of this position: Billy Graham, *The Holy Spirit: Activating God's Power in Your Life*, Thomas Nelson, 1978

is not bound by our generalisations or our rule-making, because he treats each one of us as a special case.

It could be argued from the Bible that we are placed in Christ when we first believe in his name and that he will come to live in us when we are willing to submit to the will of the Father. Mary, the mother of Jesus received her son when she believed the angel's message and said "yes" to God.

Luke 1:38 **"I am the Lord's servant," Mary answered. "May it be to me as you have said." Then the angel left her.**

We need Mary's faith and her submission to the dynamically revealed will of God to know that Christ is in us.

2. Why, even though the Bible assures us we are in Christ and he is in us, do we find it difficult to believe this?

It appears from the biblical record, that our position in Christ and his presence in us are not always perceived.

1 John 3:24 **Those who obey his commands live in him, and he in them. And this is how we know that he lives in us: We know it by the Spirit he gave us.**

This verse indicates that it is the Holy Spirit who gives us the experiential evidence that Christ lives in us. God gives us experiences to validate what his Word says, but we must start with the Word. He asks us to believe that Jesus lives in us, *as the Scripture has said*, and to act accordingly, i.e. to live as he did when he was on earth. Then we will experience his presence and see the miracles that he did flowing from us in the power of the Holy Spirit.

3. How can we open ourselves up more to Christ working through us?

The key factor seems to be our focus – is it on ourselves and what we can do for him *or* is it on him. Bill Johnson was asked what had led to the revival that they had been seeing in Redding for more than 15 years and he said, "Abandonment in worship". This is the top half of the drawing where those in Christ direct their affection to the Father, through the Son in the power of the Holy Spirit. The more heavenly-minded we are, the more space opens up in us on earth for Jesus to fill.

4. How does all of this relate to the baptism of the Holy Spirit?

As noted above, in the 20th Century, parts of the world-wide church focussed strongly on the baptism of the Holy Spirit. In the 21st Century, God wants to build on all that has been discovered about the baptism of the Holy Spirit, but with him there is always more…

- John the Baptist said it was Jesus who would baptise us in the Holy Spirit; therefore Jesus' presence with us is essential to receive this baptism.

- Jesus' ministry on earth did not start until he was baptised in the Spirit, we can expect the same to be true for us. The baptism empowered him and gave him a hot-line to the Father, but he still needed to live the life that he had come to earth for. The Gospels record the life and work of Jesus in the power of the Holy Spirit; they are the 'instruction manual' for our lives.

Baptism is a one-off event that marks a transition in a person's life; there is a difference between before and after. The presence of Christ in us is an ongoing, deepening, relational experience with many facets. This is like the difference between water and wine. At the wedding in Cana, Jesus changed plain water that was applied on the outside[27] of the body to rich wine that went right inside. The baptism of the Holy Spirit is to be eagerly sought, but it is a means, not an end. If the focus of our Christian life and ministry remains there, we will miss what was most precious to the first disciples: they **had been with Jesus** (Acts 4:13).

> *This baptism with the Holy Spirit is what immerses Christ's disciples into the fullness of His life and nature and enables them to manifest the light of His life. (John 8:12)... We must give up the self-life in order to receive the Christ-life. It will be necessary to choose one or the other because we cannot serve both the flesh and the Spirit. "No one can serve two masters." (Matt. 6: 24) Only those who are willing to live wholly under the control and power of Christ's Spirit have the promise of an inner manifestation of His divine life. (John 14: 19-21; 2 Cor. 3: 17-18)*[28]

Stingless Bees

> *I had a vision from God which was about being amongst some bees and I felt very warm and comfortable with them but at the time I did not realize that these bees had no stings (no weapons) which God immediately prompted me by saying that can't you see, these bees they have no stings. I think Jesus is saying, "Lay down all your weapons at the church door you do not need them. And you will be able to come closer to me where you will find comfort and rest under my wing. There are no barriers between any of us because of what I have done on the Cross. But when you go back out through*

---

[27] See John 2:6, the water was used for ceremonial washing, not for drinking.
[28] W. Ian Thomas, The Saving Life of Christ, (London, Oliphants Ltd., 1961), pages 2...8

the door you will need to put on your armour of God. "[29]

Phil did not know that we had given permission for a colony of stingless ('mason') bees (*osmia bicornis*) to be put in the churchyard. This is part of a scheme to re-introduce this endangered species into the urban environment.

---

[29] Vision by Philip Cole, 26th May 2012

Proposal

Name change

"What's in a name?
That which we call a rose
By any other name would smell as sweet."[30]

That may be true for Shakespeare, but not for God. Names have deep significance in the Bible, firstly because words themselves are very important. God has given us the amazing gift of language so that he can speak to us and we can communicate back to him and to each other. Jesus is called 'the Word' in John's Gospel because he is God communicating to us in words, in actions and ultimately in himself. God speaks, and he listens when we speak. The creation was brought into being by the word of God (see Genesis 1), and, as the centurion knew, will always obey the command of the Son of God.

Luke 7:7 **"...But say the word, and my servant will be healed."**

In order to use the incredible power of the spoken word, we need names for things, particularly for people and places. Perhaps because of this power, God sometimes reserves to himself the authority to assign names. This was certainly true for his own name:

Exodus 3:13-15 **Moses said to God, "Suppose I go to the Israelites and say to them, 'The God of your fathers has**

---

[30] William Shakespeare, *Romeo and Juliet*, (Act 2, Scene 2)

sent me to you,' and they ask me, 'What is his name?' Then what shall I tell them?" God said to Moses, "I AM WHO I AM. This is what you are to say to the Israelites: 'I AM has sent me to you.'" God also said to Moses, "Say to the Israelites, 'The LORD, the God of your fathers—the God of Abraham, the God of Isaac and the God of Jacob—has sent me to you.' This is my name for ever, the name by which I am to be remembered from generation to generation."

The name of God's son was also specifically given to both Joseph and Mary, and we know that there is power in the name Jesus:

> Philippians 2:10-11 ...at the name of Jesus every knee should bow, in heaven and on earth and under the earth, and every tongue confess that Jesus Christ is Lord, to the glory of God the Father.

Throughout history, most have been named by their parents, but God changed the names of a few very significant people:

- Abram → Abraham,
- Sarai → Sarah
- Jacob → Israel
- Simon → Peter

In each case, the name change indicated that the individual had been chosen to fulfil a new role in the life of God's people. Abraham, Sarah and Israel were to be the ancestors of the race that would produce the Messiah. Peter was chosen to be a foundation[31] for the church, the role that he so clearly demonstrated on the Day of Pentecost.

---

[31] Ephesians 2:20

Our interest in the subject of name changes by God came from a day (14th February 2013) when we believe God called a fast and an assembly. The Bible passage that guided the day was this:

Isaiah 62:1-7

> For Zion's sake I will not keep silent,
>   for Jerusalem's sake I will not remain quiet,
>   till her righteousness shines out like the dawn,
>   her salvation like a blazing torch.
> The nations will see your righteousness,
>   and all kings your glory;
>   you will be called by a new name
>   that the mouth of the Lord will bestow.
> You will be a crown of splendour in the Lord's hand,
>   a royal diadem in the hand of your God.
> No longer will they call you Deserted,
>   or name your land Desolate.
> But you will be called Hephzibah,
> and your land Beulah
> for the Lord will take delight in you,
>   and your land will be married.
> As a young man marries a maiden,
>   so will your builder marry you;
>   as a bridegroom rejoices over his bride,
>   so will your God rejoice over you.
> I have posted watchmen on your walls, O Jerusalem;
>   they will never be silent day or night.
> You who call on the LORD, give yourselves no rest,
>   and give him no rest till he establishes Jerusalem
>   and makes her the praise of the earth.

We believed that God was telling us that we should call on him, and give neither him nor ourselves rest until he establishes our 'city'. Going back a few verses, we find that the Lord's fulfilment of this will be by him becoming our bridegroom, and consequently changing our name; *Hephzibah* means 'my delight is in her' and *Beulah* means 'married'.

This passage was used in the first book written at HTBV in recent years; Laura Barratt described a vision:

> *In July 2009 God gave me a vision of this. I had this picture of myself walking along a beach. As I was walking I could see Jesus walking in front of me; when I saw it was Jesus I started speeding up to get closer to him, and I was trying to show him that I wanted to be so close to him walking in his ways and that I was right behind him following his every move. I knew that he wanted me to follow him and watch what he was doing. As I was walking right behind him he put his hand out; and I knew he was beckoning me to go and walk alongside him. I felt the Lord say to me "Do not walk behind me, but alongside me. Give me your hand, for you do not have to look at the back of me, come and walk beside me. For I am the bridegroom and you are the bride. Walk beside me beautiful bride, for this is the season I am leading my church into. It is a new season. It is time for the bride and the bridegroom to walk alongside one another. It is time for my church to be visible." God is calling his church to be intimate with him. For us to walk hand in hand with him. For us to be joined with him hand in hand. [32]*

During the day of assembly and fasting, Derek McCormack was given the two words 'alabaster' and 'Bethany', and we realised that this latter name was a new name from God for our fellowship. The rest of this book will explore the meaning and implications of this renaming, but to summarise:

- Jesus was anointed by Mary breaking an alabaster jar of nard—an act of extravagant worship (Mark 14:3, John 12:3)

---

[32] Richard Spencer, Laura Barratt, *Pursuing the Presence*, Chapter 7

- Jesus felt at home (Matthew 21:7, Matthew 26:6, Mark 11:11-12)
- Jesus was honoured (John 12:2)
- Jesus was listened to (Luke 10:39)
- New life was given—the raising of Lazarus (John 11)
- Jesus returned to heaven:

> Luke 24:50-51 **When he had led them out to the vicinity of Bethany, he lifted up his hands and blessed them. While he was blessing them, he left them and was taken up into heaven.**

The reference to the Ascension is a confirmation of the new name, as this exact scene is portrayed in the main stained glass window in the chancel of the church (where we met on 14th February), and not the alternative description of the Ascension in Acts 2.

Perhaps the clearest confirmation that Jesus was giving us a new name came just a week or so later. In our newsletter, we reprinted (with permission) an interesting 'blog' from the American writer Frank Viola. The very next week the blog announced a new book, which Frank Viola has stated is his 'life's work'. This book is entitled 'God's Favorite Place on Earth' and is all about... **Bethany**!

The Lord's Heartbeat: The Lord is looking for a group of people who will give Him first place in their lives, including their time. He's after a people who are willing to do whatever is necessary to satisfy His heart. In short, He's looking for a people who will love and worship Him extravagantly. The gospel narrative of Bethany symbolizes all of these things. God wants every Christian to be a Bethany, and He wants every church to be a Bethany —an

48

extended family made up of sisters and brothers who waste themselves upon Jesus and satisfy His heart."[33]

'One thing'

Luke 10:38-42 (NKJV) Now it happened as they went that He entered a certain village; and a certain woman named Martha welcomed Him into her house. And she had a sister called Mary, who also sat at Jesus' feet and heard His word. But Martha was distracted with much serving, and she approached Him and said, "Lord, do You not care that my sister has left me to serve alone? Therefore tell her to help me." And Jesus answered and said to her, "Martha, Martha, you are worried and troubled about many things. But one thing is needed, and Mary has chosen that good part, which will not be taken away from her."

The one thing that Mary did was to hear Jesus' word. She was like the centurion who knew the power of Jesus' words.

Luke 7:7 ...But say the word, and my servant will be healed.

Bethany is a place to draw aside and hear Jesus speaking to us, to know his direction and for him to change the world. And he wants to speak through us, but first we need to listen to him, and to believe him.

Church should be a place to spend time at Jesus' feet, receiving all the revelation that he wants to give us, where this has absolute priority over the 'many things' that seem to be needed. It is not the eternal word that is recorded in the Scripture, but the immediate, the specific word for today. And the example of the centurion shows that Jesus does not need to be physically present for his word to have a profound effect.

---

[33] Frank Viola, *God's Favorite Place on Earth*, please see Bibliography.

Bringing people to faith is a primary purpose of the church, and the Bible tells us that people's ears need to be opened by the direct word of Jesus:

> Romans 10:17 …faith comes from hearing the message, and the message is heard through the word of Christ.

The Greek word here translated 'word' is *rhema*, which is generally used for the immediate, spoken, prophetic word, as opposed to *logos*, the eternal, unchanging, written or embodied word. However, Jesus' told Martha that all the revelations that we receive from him will last for ever. He said it again:

> Luke 21:33 "Heaven and earth will pass away, but my words will never pass away."

Every communication we have ever received from Jesus has more substance than the whole of creation.

There are only a few occasions in the New Testament where we hear the voice of the Father speaking from heaven. One of these in on the Mount of Transfiguration:

> Matthew 17:5 While *Jesus* was still speaking, a bright cloud enveloped them, and a voice from the cloud said, "This is my Son, whom I love; with him I am well pleased. Listen to him!"

The substance of the Father's words was a repetition of what was heard at Jesus' baptism[34], but they conclude with a command Mary would have been only too happy to obey.

So the 'one thing' needed is listening to Jesus.

---

[34] Matthew 3:17

The First Church

In the United States, as you drive through most towns you will see signs outside churches naming them as 'First Methodist Church' or 'First Baptist Church', etc., but where was the first church of all? It is usually asserted that the church started on the Day of Pentecost in Jerusalem, but what was going on in Bethany, weeks or months before, has all the characteristics of a local church[35].

The First Church of Bethany was based at the house of the three siblings: Martha, Mary and Lazarus, but there were others, including those who were at the dinner given in Jesus' honour described in John 12. Jesus had told Peter earlier what would constitute a church:

> Matthew 16:13-19 **When Jesus came to the region of Caesarea Philippi, he asked his disciples, "Who do people say the Son of Man is?" They replied, "Some say John the Baptist; others say Elijah; and still others, Jeremiah or one of the prophets." "But what about you?" he asked. "Who do you say I am?" Simon Peter answered, "You are the Christ, the Son of the living God." Jesus replied, "Blessed are you, Simon son of Jonah, for this was not revealed to you by man, but by my Father in heaven. And I tell you that you are Peter, and on this rock I will build my church, and the gates of Hades will not overcome it. I will give you the keys of the kingdom of heaven; whatever you bind on earth will be bound in heaven, and whatever you loose on earth will be loosed in heaven."**

---

[35] It could be argued that the twelve apostles were the first church, in which case Bethany was the first church in a fixed locality.

The first (and perhaps the most important) characteristic of a church is that it is a community of people who know who Jesus is and are willing to declare it:

John 11:27 ...*Martha* told him, "I believe that you are the Christ, the Son of God, who was to come into the world."

This revelation spoken out by Peter and again by Martha is the foundation that Jesus needs to build his church. The second characteristic of the church is summed up in the enigmatic phrase '**the gates of Hades will not prevail against it**' (as in the Authorised Version). There has been much debate as to what Jesus meant by these words; the key to understanding is the realization that Hades is the place of the dead, corresponding to Sheol in the Old Testament. This is not Hell, the place of eternal fire; Hades is a more neutral word. Therefore, the gates (plural) of Hades are the different ways that we pass from being alive to being dead: generally sicknesses and injuries. The first promise that Jesus gave to Peter for the church is that it would be a place of healing and of resurrection; as a church we should expect to be able to heal and to raise the dead. This is exactly what happened in Bethany.

Jesus said that the third characteristic of the church would be:

Matthew 16:19 "I will give you the keys of the kingdom of heaven; whatever you bind on earth will be bound in heaven, and whatever you loose on earth will be loosed in heaven."

This found its fulfilment at Bethany, Jesus made the connection between earth and heaven clear when he spoke to the Father, and when he commanded that Lazarus should go free.

John 11:41-44 So they took away the stone. Then Jesus looked up and said, "Father, I thank you that you have heard me. I knew that you always hear me, but I said this for the benefit of the people standing here, that they may believe that you sent me." When he had said this, Jesus called in a loud voice, "Lazarus, come out!" The dead man came out, his hands and feet wrapped with strips of linen, and a cloth around his face. Jesus said to them, "Take off the grave clothes and let him go."

Other aspects of church life can be found in the Biblical accounts about Bethany:

Fellowship and eating together

John 12:2 Here a dinner was given in Jesus' honour. Martha served, while Lazarus was among those reclining at the table with him.

All corporate meals should be like this – with Jesus as the guest of honour, and with us serving and eating with him.

Teaching

Luke 10:39 She had a sister called Mary, who sat at the Lord's feet listening to what he said.

We should always be eager to hear from Jesus, and we know he can speak through all the members of his body.

Worship

John 12:3 Then Mary took about a pint of pure nard, an expensive perfume; she poured it on Jesus' feet and wiped his feet with her hair. And the house was filled with the fragrance of the perfume.

The worship that Jesus appreciates is costly, personal, intimate, expressed physically, affects others, spontaneous, non-programmed, comes from the heart.

Evangelism

John 11:45 Therefore many of the Jews who had come to visit Mary, and had seen what Jesus did, put their faith in him.

We don't usually think of Mary of Bethany as an evangelist but she clearly is one. Her 'evangelistic strategy' is simply to invite people to where Jesus is at work. This helps us to see how Jesus is calling the church today to reach out into the world. Most importantly, our churches need to be places where Jesus' body is under full control of its head and where no constraints are put on his activity in us, with us and through us. The only other requirement is for people to 'visit' us, and this does not just mean on a Sunday in a particular building. We tend to put all of our attention on arranging ways that people can visit with us, but without the manifest presence of Jesus at the heart of his people, we are just niche marketing; i.e. doing the 'things of men'[36]

We also see something in Bethany that has been the experience of the church down the centuries, persecution:

John 12:10 So the chief priests made plans to kill Lazarus as well, for on account of him many of the Jews were going over to Jesus and putting their faith in him.

---

[36] Matthew 16:23

The Children of the Father, the Bride of the Son

Bethany is the place where we discover what a relationship with Jesus really means. We meet three people who we are repeatedly told that Jesus loved[37]. We find there the prototype church.

> Ephesians 5:28-32 28 ...husbands ought to love their wives as their own bodies. He who loves his wife loves himself. 29 After all, no one ever hated his own body, but he feeds and cares for it, just as Christ does the church— 30 for we are members of his body. 31 "For this reason a man will leave his father and mother and be united to his wife, and the two will become one flesh." 32 This is a profound mystery—but I am talking about Christ and the church.

The New Testament writers speak of the church as the Bride of Christ, and Paul, in the passage above, goes as far as to quote from the account of the first union of a man and woman in the Bible:

> Genesis 2: 21-25 21 So the LORD God caused the man to fall into a deep sleep; and while he was sleeping, he took one of the man's ribs and closed up the place with flesh. 22 Then the LORD God made a woman from the rib he had taken out of the man, and he brought her to the man. 23 The man said, "This is now bone of my bones and flesh of my flesh; she shall be called 'woman', for she was taken out of man." 24 For this reason a man will leave his father and mother and be united to his wife, and they will become one flesh. 25 The man and his wife were both naked, and they felt no shame.

---

[37] John 11:3, 5 and 36

Genesis 2:24 is the Old Testament verse that is quoted most frequently in the New Testament. The use of this verse in Ephesians 5:31 includes the words 'for this reason', which, in each case, shows that what is being expressed here follows on from the previous words. In Genesis, this directly follows the creation of Eve, who was formed from a member of Adam's body by God. Adam had been animated by God breathing his life into a body that he had formed, and we presume he did the same for Eve. Genesis 2:24 is therefore speaking about the creation of new life – a man leaves the place of his creation (when his father and mother came together to conceive him) and is united with his wife to bring into being another new life – their child. The creation of Eve set the pattern for the begetting (to use the correct, but archaic word) of subsequent generations.

This helps us to understand why Paul left in the words 'for this reason' when he quoted Genesis 2:24. He precedes this with the words 'for we are members of his body'. The starting point for the creation of Eve was a member of Adam's body. Later, she united with him to beget new life – Cain, Abel, Seth, and their other children. As members of Jesus' body, the church, we are united with him to bring into being new life. As Eve 'received' Adam physically, we receive Jesus spiritually:

> John 1:12-13 **Yet to all who received him, to those who believed in his name, he gave the right to become children of God – children born not of natural descent, nor of human decision or a husband's will, but born of God.**

The new beings that are created from the union of Jesus and the members of his body, the church, are born-again believers. Nicodemus seemed to half-understand this by referring to his mother's womb:

> John 3:3-6 **...Jesus declared, "I tell you the truth, no-one can see the kingdom of God unless he is born again." "How**

can a man be born when he is old?" Nicodemus asked. "Surely he cannot enter a second time into his mother's womb to be born!" Jesus answered, "I tell you the truth, no-one can enter the kingdom of God unless he is born of water and the Spirit. Flesh gives birth to flesh, but the Spirit gives birth to spirit."

The Greek word that is translated here (and in John 1) as 'born' also means 'conceived'. Jesus told Nicodemus that physical conception which involves a substance passing from father to mother (euphemistically referred to as 'water') is a picture of spiritual conception where the Holy Spirit enters into to a person. In physical conception the life of the father fuses with the life of the mother to create a new human being. In spiritual conception, the life of God fuses with human life to create a being like Jesus, still fully human, yet who shares his divine life[38].

It may seem to be stretching things to draw this parallel between the physical (or natural) and the spiritual, but Paul wrote about this explicitly:

> 1 Corinthians 15:45-49 So it is written: "The first man Adam became a living being"; the last Adam, a life-giving spirit. 46 The spiritual did not come first, but the natural, and after that the spiritual. 47 The first man was of the dust of the earth, the second man from heaven. 48 As was the earthly man, so are those who are of the earth; and as is the man from heaven, so also are those who are of heaven. 49 And just as we have borne the likeness of the earthly man, so shall we bear the likeness of the man from heaven.

Just as Adam was the origin of a new species that would be propagated by the union of male and female members of that

---

[38] 2 Peter 1:4

species, so new creatures would come into being from the union of the Son of God and ordinary human beings. Natural children have the characteristics of their parents; born-again believers carry the likeness of both their original nature and the nature of Jesus. When we come to faith in Jesus, the person we were becomes the 'mother' of who we now *are* in Christ[39].

Some more points about those who are born again:

- We have the Father as 'our father' and Jesus as our Bridegroom: the parent-child and husband-wife relationships 'in the natural' help us to understand how to love God.
- We are genuine, legitimate[40] children of God and therefore can expect an inheritance[41].

The Alabaster Jar

Mary's anointing oil was a sweet smelling fragrance, a pleasing aroma unto the Lord.

There are parallels between physical things in the Old Covenant worship and spiritual things in the New Covenant. For example,

Old Covenant worship

Numbers 28:1-2 The LORD said to Moses, 2 "Give these instructions to the people of Israel: The offerings you present as special gifts are a pleasing aroma to me; they are my food. See to it that they are brought at the appointed times and offered according to my

---

[39] John 1:12

[40] See Hebrews 12:8

[41] See Romans 8:17, Ephesians 1:18, Colossians 1:12, Hebrews 9:15,, 1 Peter 1:4

instructions."

New Covenant worship

Hebrews 13:15 Through Him, therefore, let us constantly and at all times offer up to God a sacrifice of praise, which is the fruit of lips that thankfully acknowledge and confess and glorify His name.

We read in Amos 5:21 that the offerings and religious rituals under the old way of worship were actually a stench in the nostrils of God and it was not the way God wanted to relate to man. The old way of worship was always a shadow of the good things to come, that is Christ.

Colossians 2:16-17 Therefore do not let anyone judge you by what you eat or drink, or with regard to a religious festival, a New Moon celebration or a Sabbath day. These are a shadow of the things that were to come; the reality, however, is found in Christ.

True Worship

Religious people will always try to condemn true worshippers, picking out their faults and shortcomings. But God looks at the heart. When Mary anointed Jesus at Bethany, some said that Mary was not bringing true worship to God and that giving the money from the selling of the oil was the 'right' thing to do as a follower of Jesus. These people were caught up in works-righteousness.

Mark 14:4-9 (AMP) But there were some who were moved with indignation and said to themselves, To what purpose was the ointment (perfume) thus wasted? For it was possible to have sold this [perfume] for more than 300 denarii [a labouring man's wages for a year] and to have given [the money] to the poor. And they censured and reproved her. But Jesus said, Let her alone; why are you troubling her?

She has done a good and beautiful thing to Me [praiseworthy and noble]. For you always have the poor with you, and whenever you wish you can do good to them; but you will not always have Me. She has done what she could; she came beforehand to anoint My body for the burial. And surely I tell you, wherever the good news (the Gospel) is proclaimed in the entire world, what she has done will be told in memory of her.

Worship is not about 'doing' for Jesus, although good works will be a fruit. It is about being in union with him. God created us to be in relationship with Him. We were created for his glory[42] and pleasure. We are not 'human doings', we are human beings!

In Luke chapter 10, Mary and Martha are examples of this. Martha served and complained whilst Mary sat at Jesus' feet. Jesus said Mary has chosen the better part.

We are the earthen vessels filled with the expensive oil, which is, the Holy Spirit[43], and we can also pour out extravagant worship on Jesus.

2 Corinthians 2:14-15 (AMP) **But thanks be to God, Who in Christ always leads us in triumph [as trophies of Christ's victory] and through us spreads and makes evident the fragrance of the knowledge of God everywhere. For we are the sweet fragrance of Christ [which exhales] unto God, [discernible alike] among those who are being saved and among those who are perishing:"**

The Perfume

- Was worth about a years wages

---

[42] Isaiah 43:7

[43] 2 Corinthians 4:7 (amp)

- Made from essence of nard (spike-nard)

- The house was filled with its fragrance. On approach to the house you could smell it. We are the house!

- Was pleasing to the Lord (Heb 2:12 says Jesus through us is perfect worship) If we want to be true worshippers we must worship in spirit and truth.

- Was expensive

The anointing oil inside us is so valuable that in order for us to have it, God had to send Jesus to die in our place. The cost was so great. The cost was death on a cross. God the Father extravagantly gave worth to you and me long before we could ever think of worshipping Him. The precious promise of the Holy Spirit came through Abram all the way to the fulfilment of it through Jesus. He came to earth and was broken like the alabaster jar so that we could receive the sweet smelling fragrance of the Holy Spirit and be witnesses for Christ.

Jesus said,

John 10:10 (AMP) **"The thief comes only in order to steal and kill and destroy. I came that they may have and enjoy life, and have it in abundance (to the full, till it overflows).**

The Holy Spirit is the treasure inside us. He is our life. He is the fountain of living water that springs up out of us so that we will never thirst again.

Our real life is hidden in Christ

Colossians 3:3 **For ye are dead, and your life is hid with Christ in God.**

So where is Christ?

Ephesians 1:20 **"...that raised Christ from the dead and seated him in the place of honour at God's right hand in the heavenly realms."**

Also read Colossians 1:27

And where are we?

Ephesians 2:6 **For he raised us from the dead along with Christ and seated us with him in the heavenly realms because we are united with Christ Jesus."**

If Christ is our life how do we get this life out? How do we pour out the fragrance of Christ?

We worship Him. He has already given us His love, joy, peace, prosperity, victory in the spiritual realm. We are blessed with every spiritual blessing in the heavenly realms in Christ Jesus[44]. We are more than conquerors in him, but we won't experience his life unless we continually turn our affection towards Him, our mind, will and emotions.

Psalm 71:8 **My mouth shall be filled with Your praise and with Your honour all the day.**

Worship is a journey of continual remembrance and fixation upon Jesus.

Colossians 3:1(AV) **If ye then be risen with Christ, seek those things which are above where Christ sitteth on the right hand of God.**

The word that is translated 'seek' means 'to worship', or in a bad sense 'to plot' against life. 'to lust after', 'a strong desire', 'crave'

Colosians 3:2 **Set your affection on things above, not on**

---

[44] Ephesians 1:3

things on the earth.

'Set your affection on' means 'to exercise the mind', think upon, be careful = full of care towards. 'to savour', 'to feast upon'

How to worship?

• Let his praise be on your lips

Our words are an overflow from our heart.

Psalm 34:1 I will bless the Lord at all times; His praise shall continually be in my mouth.

Psalm 71:8 My mouth shall be filled with Your praise and with Your honour all the day.

Psalm 63:3 Because your love is better than life, my lips will glorify you.

Further study: Psalm 30:11-12, Psalm 35:27-28

It's more blessed to give than receive

2 Corinthians 9:7 talks about cheerful giving. We come to church not to get, but to give. Mary gave willingly (cheerfully). Are we living to give? That which we sow we shall also reap.

Jesus said,

Luke 6:38 (AMP) "Give, and [gifts] will be given to you; good measure, pressed down, shaken together, and running over, will they pour into [the pouch formed by] the bosom [of your robe and used as a bag]. For with the measure you deal out [with the measure you use when you confer benefits on others], it will be measured back to you."

Worship is definitely giving. God is a giver[45]. We were made in His image and likeness therefore we are also givers. Everybody loves to give in some way or other.

God has a way of making us feel more blessed when we give. Peter and John at the gate of Beautiful gave the crippled man healing to his body. I know that when God heals someone through me, I feel more blessed than if I had received healing myself! It is such a blessing to help someone in need. I believe it's because we were made in the image and likeness of God the Trinity.

The more we understand the love of God towards us, the more we will worship him.

The more we experience His grace and mercy, the more we will be compelled to worship him. His mercies are new everyday. There is always more to be thankful for. We love Him because He first loved us. Love is the greatest force. 1 Corinthians 14:1 tells us to 'pursue love.' It is the goodness of God that draws people to repentance[46]. To repent simply means to change the way you think about something or someone. As we have more and more revelation of God's love for us, we will naturally worship him in new and deeper ways.

'Lazarus, come forth!'

On 12th October 2013, some of us attended a day's teaching on prophecy at the Community Church, Wrexham, led by Nick Pengelly. During the morning, Nick encouraged us to spend a few minutes writing down whatever we believed God was saying at that moment. I retreated to the back of the hall and wrote these words:

---

[45] John 3:16

[46] Romans 2:4

By the Holy Spirit your perspective on the life of the church is being changed to align with mine. Open your heart to my work that you may see who is alive and who is dead. Who is open to the work of my Holy Spirit and who resists it. Break the power of death, cry 'Lazarus, come forth'. This is new birth. This is why Jesus delays; he is not here to fix up the church, but to resurrect it.

I found it difficult to interpret this when I wrote it, but it was amazingly confirmed when I spoke to Ann Lansdale at lunchtime, someone I had only met briefly before. Just making conversation, she recounted how God had told her a few years ago to wait until he prompted her before visiting Sainsbury's. Hours later, at the God-sanctioned time as she walked through the doors of the supermarket, she met a couple, who were going through a terrible family situation. Ann ministered to them for months, but if she had not entered the supermarket exactly when God told her to, she would never have encountered them. I showed Ann what I had written, and it blessed her as a confirmation that she really had heard God, and it also convinced me that these words really were from him.

The last line in the prophecy was at first:

This is why Jesus delayed; he was not there to fix up Lazarus, but to resurrect him.

I was clearly meant to draw a lesson from the raising of Lazarus.

The first point to note is that Jesus really loved Lazarus, we are told this three times in John 11:

Contrary to what most would think, then and now, Jesus delaying before coming to Bethany was an act of love towards his dear friend. He did not just take away Lazarus' health problem, he gave him new life. It is clear that Jesus is not interested in putting plasters on the church's problems; he wants to give it his risen life.

After some reflection, we realized he was telling us what was happening to Holy Trinity Church. The old church was dying and a new church was being born in its place. The raising of Lazarus was a better analogy than Jesus' resurrection, Lazarus died from what was wrong with him[47], he did not need human hands to kill him.

This is Jesus' perspective on the life of our church, and also why he has given us a new name – to reflect that we are living a new life[48], and connect us to the place in Israel where a community was resurrected by the raising of one man.

The prophetic word also helps us to understand what is going on within the church. We now understand the vital need for all to accept the work of the Holy Spirit in us and through us. It also helps us see that attempts to 'fix up' a church (by 'the things of men'[49]) do not have the support of its Head. Churches are often encouraged to try different techniques to attract new members, Jesus' way is to let the old die and to infuse new life into the corpse. Our job is to take away the stone and to remove the graveclothes – that is to remove what is no longer needed, but is just getting in the way of this new life.

It is an intriguing thought that Jesus came to Bethany, not just to bring new life and new birth to Lazarus, but to the community that was beginning to form in Jesus' name. It gives us the understanding that resurrection of the church today is necessary,

---

[47] This is how John 11 starts: **Now a man named Lazarus was sick. He was from Bethany, the village of Mary and her sister Martha.** (John 11:1)

[48] Romans 6:4

[49] Matthew 16:23

66

and the hope that is possible. It is clearly dependant on our faith and our courage to speak new life into what is essentially dead.

If a body is naturally dead we will observe no physical activity, if a body is spiritually dead, we will see no supernatural activity. Jesus is calling us to speak new life into parts of his body that currently are dead.

An example of this is in the conversation with Nicodemus in John 3[50]. Nicodemus was intrigued by Jesus' miracles, but he came for a reasoned theological discussion. However, he received something else, the shocking news that he needed to be born again. Jesus spoke new life into Nicodemus, not by an intellectual argument, but telling him the plain, unvarnished truth.

The church today needs to be resurrected. The dictionary definition of 'to resurrect' is 'to bring back something into use or existence that had disappeared or ended'. Jesus longs for his church to be what he always intended it to be, what it was 'at the beginning', a body that truly expresses the heart, the soul, the love, the wisdom, the nature, the personality, the power,… of its Head.

Other Postcards from Bethany

The Fig Tree – Mark 11:13-14; Mark 11:20-21

As Jesus was going out from Bethany to Jerusalem he encountered the fig tree with no fruit, which he cursed and which subsequently withered. Jesus used the withering of the tree in a lesson on the power of faith, but it is clear from the context that the fig tree was a picture of his judgment on the Jewish faith. The journey from Bethany to Jerusalem can be seen as going from the

---

[50] It is possible that this conversation happened in Bethany; Jesus was certainly in Judea at the time, see John 2:23, John 3:11.

New Covenant back into the Old Covenant. Jesus had unfinished business there, he needed to offer the sacrifice of himself in a clear fulfilment of all the Old Covenant offerings – the Passover Lamb, the Scapegoat, etc. Jesus calls us to follow him in offering ourselves, which may mean encountering religion in one form or another. Jesus needed a secure place (where he was valued, honoured and supported) to go out from; to enable him to stand against the religious spirit of his age. How much more do we need an equivalent place as we go out to face all the religions of today (including secularism, militant atheism, New Age thinking,... the list is endless)?

The Palm Sunday Donkey – Mark 11:1-7

The Palm Sunday donkey was not supplied by any of the inhabitants of Jerusalem. It came from either Bethany or the next-door village, Bethphage. Jesus' needs were not great; he just needed a young donkey on loan for a few hours, but it is the privilege of these little communities to supply everything for him.

Mark 11:3 *Jesus said, "If anyone asks you, 'Why are you doing this?' tell him, 'The Lord needs it and will send it back here shortly.'"*

To be a Bethany, a church, must continue to listen out for these words about anything: "the Lord needs it".

Resting Place in Passion Week – Mark 11:11

Jesus is the complete model for the Christian life. He shows us what human beings are capable of, empowered by the Holy Spirit and under the authority of the Father. He also shows us that we do have limitations that are not the result of our sinfulness. In the most crucial week of his life on earth, Jesus needed a place of security and comfort to retreat to. That place was Bethany.

A church called Bethany needs to be a community that will support and nurture those going through difficult times. We need to be a place of rest, particularly rest from our enemies.

My call to stipendiary ministry in the Church of England was through a passage in Exodus 33 which contains these words:

> Exodus 33:14 **The LORD replied, "My Presence will go with you, and I will give you rest."**

I began to appreciate what God meant by the first half of this promise (originally to Moses, but now also to me) when things stared happening in December 2006; but the second half has become equally real as we have discovered more and more what 'Bethany' means. It is a place where we can find rest from our enemies, we can let our guards down and we can be vulnerable to each other. The vision of the stingless bees helps us to see the importance of a place of rest (see page 43).

The Ascension – Luke 24:50

Bethany was the last place on earth that Jesus' feet touched. His choice of this location tells us more about what a 21st Century Bethany should be; it is a place where heaven and earth are connected, like Bethel in Genesis 28:11-22. It also reminds us of Jesus' words to Nathaniel:

> John 1:51 **"I tell you the truth, you shall see heaven open, and the angels of God ascending and descending on the Son of Man."**

Bethany is a place where heaven is open, where we are conscious that angels are around us, and that it is the presence of Jesus himself that makes all of this possible.

Jesus' last action on earth was to bless his followers:

> Luke 24:50-51 **When Jesus had led them out to the vicinity of Bethany, he lifted up his hands and blessed them. While**

he was blessing them, he left them and was taken up into heaven.

Bethany is therefore a place for people to experience Jesus' blessing, but also where we bless each other and the world. We are grateful to Roy and Daphne Godwin of Ffald-y-Brenin for all they have taught about the power and the glory of blessing others. Please see Roy's book, *The Grace Outpouring* in the Bibliography on page 89.

Marriage

The Resurrected, Organic Church

A book that has inspired us to believe that we are not alone in seeking a more authentic kind of local church is Frank Viola's. *Reimagining Church: Pursuing the Dream of Organic Christianity*[51]. A quotation from this book explains the term, 'organic church':

> *In the institutional church, congregants watch a religious performance once or twice a week led principally by one person (the pastor or minister), and then retreat home to live their individual Christian lives.*
>
> *By contrast, I'm using "organic church" to refer to those churches that operate according to the same spiritual principles as the church that we read about in our New Testament. The New Testament church was first and foremost organic, as are all churches that stand in its lineage. T. Austin-Sparks is the man who deserves credit for the term "organic church." He writes,*
>
> > *God's way and law of fullness is that of organic life. In the Divine order, life produces its own organism, whether it be a vegetable, animal, human or spiritual. This means that everything comes from the inside. Function, order and fruit issue from this law of life within. It was solely on this principle that what we have in the New Testament came*

---

[51] Viola, Frank, *Reimagining Church: Pursuing the Dream of Organic Christianity*, see Bibliography.

into being. Organized Christianity has entirely reversed this order.[52]

This idea of a church living by the risen life of Christ is exactly in line with the prophetic word given to us about the raising of Lazarus at Bethany. We live by the life of Jesus living in us.

Setting Jesus Free

In the early spring of 2014, Sarah Edwards discerned that Jesus was leading us into a Worship Week (i.e. gathering every evening to meet with him in praise and worship), which started on the Tuesday after Easter (22nd April). It was absolutely amazing and on the Wednesday…

I had a picture, during the quiet worship time on Wednesday evening, of a visitors' room in an American style prison - prisoner and visitor sitting on opposite sides of an unbreakable glass barrier. I was the visitor and Jesus was the prisoner. (Why it was this way round, I didn't understand) Usually in dramas of this type the two people 'touch' through the glass as the visitor is leaving and this is just what Jesus and I did. I felt I wanted more - a real touch, but this I wasn't able to do. Jesus then smiled and shook his head and the 'prison' setting disappeared and we were touching, hand to hand in open fields where there were flowers and meadows and trees and streams. I asked that if anyone knew why I was the visitor and Jesus the prisoner, could they please let me know. (Helen's explanation that Jesus put himself on 'death row' for our sake and thus broke down all the barriers)

---

[52] T. Austin-Sparks, Words of Wisdom and Revelation (Corinna, ME: Three Brothers, 2000), 49; quoted in Frank Viola, *Reimagining Church: Pursuing the Dream of Organic Christianity* (Introduction), David C. Cook, 2012

Later while sitting and thinking about this I felt that Jesus spoke to me saying that Visitation and Habitation were a two-way thing. Chris Overstreet had spoken about Jesus wanting, not just a visitation but a habitation - but Jesus was pointing out that we just 'visit' maybe for an hour once a week or once a month (like prison visiting hours) yet we can actually 'habit' with him since he has made this possible for us. We need to choose to spend that depth of time with him that constitutes habiting/living with him, instead of just visiting occasionally.

Alison Kelly

This is specifically a word for the church. 'Normal' church actually imprisons Jesus by applying human-created formulas, methods and traditions. Congregations come to visit him weekly, or less frequently, but never get close to him. In contrast, he has been leading us into a kind of church where we are 'in habitation' with him, and therefore our fellowship with him has no barrier or constraints. The Chris Overstreet prophecy (please see page 19) that we were focusing on that Wednesday night, included these words: "God wants to do a visitation, not just a visitation but a habitation in this place, where His presence becomes the theme in this church."

The Pharisees wanted to constrain Jesus by the Jewish Law, the Romans by their law and the people by wanting a king. But Jesus cannot be limited and he has to be in charge. He comes to give us freedom, but firstly we have to give him freedom. Jesus was willing to experience the worst possible constraint of being nailed to a cross, wrapped up in graveclothes and put in a tomb with a large stone at the entrance. He loves his people so much that he will allow them to constrain him, but if we want an unconstrained relationship with him, we have to set him free.

The New Testament Model for Local Church Leadership

As we read through the New Testament we have plenty of material to help us see Jesus' heart for the organisation (or better, the organism) of his body.

- In the Gospels we only have one significant reference to the church in Matthew 16:18, although Jesus' words and actions with the twelve Apostles provide many valuable insights about church leadership. Also, as we have seen, the community at Bethany show us the first church in a fixed place.
- The Book of Acts tells us much about the church in Jerusalem, which seems to be relatively free of the problems which arose in later churches, e.g. Corinth.
- Most of the Epistles are written to a church or a group of churches. It is particularly instructive to study Paul's interaction with the churches he planted and how he helped them deal with the issues they faced. It is also good to read the insights that he had into the glorious purpose God has for the church.
- The Book of Revelation contains seven letters from Jesus to individual churches in Asia (now Turkey). All of what he says to them is still relevant to us today.

The problem we face in seeking to return to the New Testament model of church is that we are dealing with nearly two thousand years of additions, deletions, amendments, etc., as the surrounding cultures have had their impact on the nature and practices of churches. As Frank Viola and George Barna pointed out in *Pagan Christianity*[53], a remarkable proportion of the

---

[53] Frank Viola, George Barn, *Pagan Christianity? Exploring the Roots of our Church Practices*, Barna Books, 2002

practices of institutional churches originate in the pagan environments that the church has found itself down the centuries. I was shocked to realise, on reading this book, how much of what seems to be essential in church life started out the Roman world of the $2^{nd} - 4^{th}$ Centuries.

If we confine ourselves to the pages of the New Testament in seeking the resurrection of the body of Christ, an interesting picture emerges. There are many ways this can be described, but we believe the following is a reasonably faithful summary of what the New Testament says.

Two Kinds of Leadership

It may be an over-simplification, but New Testament churches seem to have two kinds of leadership, seen clearly when the council in Jerusalem wrote a letter which started with these words:

> Acts 15:23 ... 'The apostles and elders, your brothers, To the Gentile believers in Antioch, Syria and Cilicia: Greetings...'

Repeatedly, this chapter refers to Apostles and Elders.

Apostles

When Jesus chose the twelve, he 'designated them Apostles'[54]. He did not use any title from the Old Testament, such as priest, prophet, patriarch, etc., but a new term to indicate that their role in the New Covenant would have no equivalent in the Old. The word means someone who is sent out on behalf of someone else with a message. We read of what they did after Pentecost in the Acts of the Apostles, and we also read that others were also given this title.

---

[54] Luke 6:13

These include people like Paul, who never met Jesus 'in the flesh'. Apostles and apostolic ministries can be identified by signs and wonders[55], and by being witnesses of the risen Jesus[56].

The role, work and nature of an apostle can be discerned by from the examples of Peter and Paul. On the Day of Pentecost, Peter stood before the people and explained what was going on. He started with what the Holy Spirit was doing (rushing wind, tongues of fire, people praising God in different languages) and connected this to what had been prophesied in the Bible, showing **"this is that"**[57]. I believe the primary purpose of an apostolic ministry is to bring Spirit and Word together, to give all of us confidence that we have an understanding what God is saying and doing at any point in time.

Apostles live in relationship with the church(es) they are ministering to. It is good to read Paul's epistles, not just for what they teach, but to see Paul's relationship with the body of each church – this is a guide for anyone called into local church leadership. Apostolic leadership is a big subject, but some points are obvious:

- Paul writes from a revealed vision for the local church in its current circumstances.

- While being very direct sometimes in individual situations, Paul never dictates; he always seeks to persuade using theology, revelation, reason and scripture.

---

[55] 2 Corinthians 12;12

[56] Acts 1:22

[57] Acts 2:16

76

- In every case, when he is writing to a local church, he writes to the whole church, not to a leadership caste. He does not need his messages to be interpreted or expanded by any intermediary. Paul never raised someone up to replace him in a church when he moved on. He was always confident that Jesus would guide his Body without the need for an ordained successor.

- He is not a consultant; he cares passionately about each church and its people, especially that they will deepen their relationship with God, through Jesus in the power of the Holy Spirit.

- Whilst caring passionately for the people of the churches that he had a hand in planting, Paul was prepared to leave each church, confident that Jesus would continue to build his church[58] without Paul's physical presence.

Elders

The New Testament uses a number of terms which are usually translated 'overseer' ('bishop'), 'elder' ('presbyter'), 'minister' ('deacon'), 'pastor' ('shepherd'). Countless words have been written analysing the epistles of the New Testament in an attempt to determine the exact role and function of each of these offices, if that is what they are. Some Christian denominations find their identity in a particular understanding of how these roles are to be exercised and the qualifications and training required by those who fulfil them.

---

[58] Matthew 16:18

My reading of the New Testament is that these titles are somewhat synonymous and interchangeable. For example:

1 Peter 5:1 -4 **To the elders among you, I appeal as a fellow-elder, a witness of Christ's sufferings and one who also will share in the glory to be revealed: Be shepherds of God's flock that is under your care, serving as overseers— not because you must, but because you are willing, as God wants you to be; not greedy for money, but eager to serve; not lording it over those entrusted to you, but being examples to the flock. And when the Chief Shepherd appears, you will receive the crown of glory that will never fade away.**

Let us, like Acts 15, use the term 'elder' to refer to all who are called into the ministries covered by these terms. If we make this generalisation, we see that all churches need a group of people of lengthy experience, excellent character, decent lifestyle and good reputation to take responsibility for the day-to-day affairs of the church[59].

The problem is that, in most denominations, this is all that is expected from church leaders. The whole business of hearing from the Head and determining what he is directing the Body to do has been lost. Churches need both apostles and elders, even if, as in Peter's case in the Bible passage above, one person may take on both roles at times.

It may seem a recipe for disaster to have two leadership groups in one organisation; many would say that it is inevitable that these groups will clash over who really is in charge. The New Testament does not endorse this, because a church is not an organisation but

---

[59] See especially 1 Timothy 3:1-13

an organism, and its Head is neither of these groups but Jesus himself.

Therefore, each church that aspires to live and work like those described in the New Testament needs elders *and* apostles, the former to take responsibility for ongoing ministry and the stewardship of resources, and the latter to ensure that the whole body is listening to and responding to its Head. In the Anglican context, the defined roles of churchwardens and PCC (Parochial Church Council) members fit reasonably well with the New Testament idea of elders (and overseers), but it is necessary to add the Apostolic function, and this is where Ephesians 4:11 is so helpful.

From Apostle to Apostolic Team

It is clear from the Book of Acts and from the epistles that Paul and the other church-planting apostles did not see the need to set up any mechanism to reproduce themselves. We see no evidence of that when Paul moved on from a church he had established, that he left a single leader 'in charge'.

Of all Paul's letters, the Book of Ephesians is the one that gives us the clearest view of a First Century church. It is often remarked, that it is the only letter that does not address any specific problems. It is not surprising therefore that this letter contains a description of what a church needs when its founder is no longer a permanent resident – what can best be described as an apostolic team.

> Ephesians 4:7-13 But to each one of us grace has been given as Christ apportioned it. This is why it says: "When he ascended on high, he led captives in his train and gave gifts to men." (What does "he ascended" mean except that he also descended to the lower, earthly regions? He who descended is the very one who ascended higher than

all the heavens, in order to fill the whole universe.) It was he who gave some to be apostles, some to be prophets, some to be evangelists, and some to be pastors and teachers, to prepare God's people for works of service, so that the body of Christ may be built up until we all reach unity in the faith and in the knowledge of the Son of God and become mature, attaining to the whole measure of the fullness of Christ.

Paul was very emphatic about his calling as an apostle, but as we read through the Acts of the Apostles, we see him fulfilling all the five-fold ministries; but he does not expect his extraordinary multi-faceted gifting to be reproduced in other individuals[60]. Rather his solution for longer-term apostolic leadership is a team that brings these giftings together:

- Apostles: As noted above, Peter, on the Day of Pentecost, shows an apostle's primary purpose is to discern the actions of the Holy Spirit and to relate them to the revelation already received (often through the use of the Bible).
- Prophets: God raises up individuals who can receive and speak out his direct revelations, which need to be tested and applied (by the apostles).
- Evangelists: Every church needs those who have been given a burden for those outside the body.
- Pastors: Similarly, we need people whose gifting turns their thoughts, words and actions towards the needs of those within the fellowship.
- Teachers: Finally, the team needs individuals whose giftings lead them to ensure that the body has a sound understanding of the eternal truths revealed in the Bible.

---

[60] With the possible exception of other church-planters like Timothy.

Mutual Edification

One of the main characteristics of an organic church identified by Frank Viola is what he terms 'mutual edification'[61]. This is where the focus is not on an appointed preacher (or even a team of preachers), but on the preference that Jesus clearly has, to speak through every member of his body.

1 Corinthians 12 is a chapter that has been poured over many times, especially by those in the Pentecostal and Charismatic movements. It starts with probably the clearest explanation in the Bible of spiritual gifts, moves on to talk about the analogy of the Body of Christ to the human body and returns to the subject of gifts in the last few verses. The section on the body is often considered on its own (especially in Sunday school classes), but it is important to consider its context when studying any passage. It is clear that the different members of Christ's body with their different gifts correspond to the parts of a human body with their very different functions, but it also clear that the mutual support of the members (using their supernatural gifts) is vital to the healthy functioning of the body as a whole. Also, this verse is crucial:

> 1 Corinthians 12:8 **For to one is given by the Spirit ~~the~~ word of wisdom; to another ~~the~~ word of knowledge by the same Spirit;...**

The two definite articles have been crossed out because they are not there in the original Greek. This implies that words of wisdom and words of knowledge are not gifts possessed by certain individuals on a semi-permanent basis, but are can be given to any member at any time. See also the 'Bread from Heaven' vision, page 17.

---

[61] Romans

It is clear that a vital component of a healthy organic church is the mutual sharing of revelation; both between individuals and from individuals to the body as a whole.

Burn for Jesus

The Apostle Paul was burning hot for Jesus Christ. He was in this thing no matter what the consequences, even to the death. Jesus promised that if we want to live a godly life we would suffer persecution. We read of Pauls **'light afflictions'**[62] for the sake of the gospel and realise that the trials we go through in the western world regarding persecution for Christ's name sake, are often pale in comparison to what these first apostles went through. A life lived in all-out surrender to Jesus is a life that will bring persecution, but be of good cheer, he has 'overcome the world'[63]. The rewards in this life and especially in the life to come far outweigh any suffering we may go through. What would the world be like if every follower of Jesus Christ didn't care so much about other people's opinions of them, but only about what God says of them? The world would be radically changed in an amazingly short space of time. Fear does not need to hold us back. When we are mindful of God's perfect love for us, all fear melts away. We have been given a spirit of love, joy and a sound mind. We can do all things through Christ who strengthens us and nothing is impossible with God.

In the summer of 2013 I believe the Lord spoke to me about building his church. The imagery He used was that of lighting a BBQ. In order for the BBQ to burn well we need to start with a few coals and get them burning hot. You cannot have all the coals fully burning bright at the beginning; it takes time for the fire to spread.

---

[62] 2 Corinthians 4:17

[63] John 16:33

It needs one or two that are on fire to influence one by one, the other coals. Before you know it the whole BBQ is well on its way to fulfilling its purpose. I believe that this picture clearly demonstrates what the Bible talks about in Ephesians:

> Ephesians 4:11-16 ...And He Himself gave some to be apostles, some prophets, some evangelists, and some pastors and teachers, for the quipping of the saints for the work of the ministry, for the edifying of the body of Christ, till we all come to the unity of the faith and of the knowledge of the Son of God, to a perfect man, to the measure of the stature of the fullness of Christ: that we should no longer be children, tossed to and fro and carried about with every wind of doctrine, by the trickery of men, in the cunning craftiness of deceitful plotting, but, speaking the truth in love, may grow up in all things into Him who is the head-Christ-from whom the whole body, joined and knit together by what every joint supplies, according to the effective working by which every part does its share, cause growth of the body for the edifying of itself in love.....

The five-fold ministry has a mandate to equip God's people to do the same works and greater. For example, an apostle is to train and equip people to do the work of an apostle. An evangelist is to train and equip people to do the work of an evangelist. The people that are trained and equipped then teach and train others. This is discipleship! In all this, the edifying of the body in love is of uttermost importance. Jesus Christ was lacking in no gift. To say that Jesus had the 'gift of healing' would be a gross understatement, yet when we speak of ourselves we may say that we have a certain special gift, not realising that we actually have the fullness of Christ. We do not need a double portion because He is our portion. We may not be experiencing all God has for us but we know that we have the same spirit that did all the miracles through Jesus. We do not have a little bit of the Holy Spirit, or even our own version of the Holy Spirit, we have the exact same Spirit that raised Jesus from the dead. The Holy Spirit in you has worked thousands of year's worth of signs, wonders and miracles. We have received the same passionate fire that burns in the eyes of Jesus Christ.

Mathew 5:16 **"In the same way, let your light shine before others, that they may see your good deeds and glorify your Father in heaven."**

We do not need worry about trying to 'make' something good happen. We rest in knowing God's love for us and the good fruit will be a natural product of who we are in Him. An apple tree does not need to work hard to produce apples; it is a natural thing that occurs because of the seed that was planted. In the same way, when we have the seed of God growing in us, we bear fruit because of who we are, not in order to live up to certain standards. Ephesians 4:15-16 seems to say that the body of Christ, the church, is joined and knit together by Christ himself, but at the same time saying that it is by what every joint supplies that the body is joined and knit together. This first appeared to me as a contradiction, is it Christ or us? Now I see that it is Christ in and through us that causes the body to be joined and knit together. It is each member operating from the indwelling life of Christ. Verse 16 goes on to say that it is according to the effective working by which every part does its share that causes the body to grow, for the edifying of itself in love.

An Organic Church in an Institution

In *Reimaging Church*, Frank Viola contrasts 'organic church' with 'institutional church' and points out how different they are. We agree with him that it is does not seem possible to change an institutional church into an organic expression of church by a series of small steps, as the Theory of Evolution might suggest. Rather, our experience has been that you need to let the institutional elements of church die off (they will do this if they are not artificially fertilized[64]). Only then can Jesus bring new life, to the extent that we witness resurrection.

However, we have found that there are some aspects of the organisation of which we are a part (in our case, the Church of England) that are of benefit even to the new, organic church.

Oversight and Accountability

Although there is only one head of all local churches, it is still valuable for all individuals and groups of people to have some human authority to whom they are accountable. Even if this oversight is never directly brought into play, it is still important that there is a place that outsiders can bring grievances, where issues affecting those outside the body can be dealt with.

The Church of England was birthed in the Reformation. The Reformers reacted against the heavyweight control exercised by the Roman Catholic hierarchy and gave each minister what is called the 'freehold' of his church. This has meant that, ever since the 16th Century, the leadership of each local Anglican Church has had considerable freedom to follow their 'conscience'[65] in matters of doctrine and worship while keeping within the 'historic formularies of the Church of England'. This freedom is exercised within their accountability to their bishop. If the relationship between minster/church and bishop is based on Christian love and respect then this provides an oversight which has to be created from scratch by independent local churches.

---

[64] The use of the word 'organic' seems particularly appropriate here!

[65] Using the term 'conscience' in the same way that Martin Luther did in his famous 'Here I stand...' speech at the Diet of Wurms.

Continuity with the Past

Lazarus was still Lazarus after he rose from the dead. He must have been transformed in ways that even non-believers could recognise, because the chief priests were planning kill him as well as Jesus[66], but he would have been able to remember encounters with Jesus before this crucial event[67]. As long as we focus on those times in the past when God was genuinely at work in us and with us, then this continuity can give us a valuable foundation on which to build for the future.

"Jesus wants to lead his church directly"

This book is the record of a conversation of a local church with her Lord; but because this conversation has extended over a number of years, the book also tells about what has happened as we have walked and talked with him. This is the way Jesus worked with the twelve, the seventy-two, the other disciples and the inhabitants of Bethany. The truth of who we are in Christ, and, far more importantly, who he is in us, is something that we are still growing into.

So where are we at this point in time? Whatever we write will always be a snapshot, because as the journey continues, fresh manna is being received all the time, we still see 'through a glass, darkly' (1 Corinthians 13:12, AV), but we have come a long way; and the revelations received to date have had profound transformational effects. We know now that Jesus wants so much

---

[66] John 12:10

[67] For example, when Jesus came to his sister's house as recorded in Luke 10:38-42

more for each local church; more than anything any kind of institutional church structure can deliver.

Ultimately, the transformation of each human being happens through encounters with Jesus. A local church is to be a place of encounter. Each member's responsibility and joy is to seek this for themselves and for others. The accounts of the village of Bethany that we read in the Gospels, show us how to be part of the Father's glorious purpose for his Son and for his church

> Ephesians 1:22-23 ...**God placed all things under his feet and appointed him to be head over everything for the church, which is his body, the fullness of him who fills everything in every way.**

Bethany in Judea was uniquely a place where Jesus was welcomed, loved, honoured, listened to and obeyed. The inhabitants individually and corporately put him at the centre of their lives and he responded by returning again and again to this little community. It was not a place for religious ritual, for seeking positions of power or for scholarly, intellectual debate; but for simply hanging out with Jesus and seeing the power of God manifested through him.

Bethany today is to be a place where Jesus is at home, where the things he hates have been cast aside; and where the things he loves can be enjoyed by all: worship, fellowship... simply loving him.

Jesus is calling each local church to be a Bethany; that longs above everything just to be with him. A fellowship that is prepared to wait for him to come into their midst (as Martha and Mary did when Lazarus died), that puts all their faith in him (and not in any of the 'things of men'), and is obedient to his word ("move the stone", "take off the grave-clothes").

Then, and only then, can Jesus return, bringing the new heaven and the new earth; when his body (the world-wide church) has grown up to be with her Bridegroom.

Conclusion

Let's give the last word to a recent visiting speaker:

What an honor and a pleasure to minister in your congregation! I absolutely love Holy Trinity... they people are so beautiful and so hungry for all of God. :-) I always love to come and be a part of how God is moving at your church. Your worship is the BEST! I loooooooove to worship at your church. It is so powerful, anointed, Holy, unique, Rhema, alive and deep! I couldn't dream of better worship! The angels are truly among us at your church. Thank you again for always inviting me. It is truly an honor. :-)[68]

---

[68] Erica Gismegian, 28th October 2014

Bibliography

Seminal Works

A number of books have been vital in understanding the revelations we have received:

Watchman Nee, *The Normal Christian Life*, Tyndale, 1957

CS Lewis, *Mere Christianity* (especially Book IV)' Godfrey Bles, 1952

W. Ian Thomas, *The Saving Life of Christ*, Oliphants, 1961

Frank Viola, *Reimagining Church: Pursuing the Dream of Organic Christianity*. David C. Cook, 2008

Frank Viola, *God's Favorite Place on Earth*, David C. Cook, 2013

Other Books

Frank Viola, *Finding Organic Church: A Comprehensive Guide to Starting and Sustaining Authentic Christian Communities* David C Cook, 2009

Roy Godwin, Dave Roberts, *The Grace Outpouring: Blessing Others Through Prayer*, David C. Cook, 2008

All books by Bill Johnson and Kris Vallotton, especially:

Kris Vallotton, *Heavy Rain,* Regal Books, 2010

Chris Overstreet, *A Practical Guide to Evangelism—Supernaturally,* Destiny Image, 2011

Torben Søndergaard, *The Last Reformation,* Laurus Books, 2013